# A STEP BY STEP GUIDE ON HOW TO START AND GROW A BUSINESS: A PROFESSIONAL TRAINING FOR BUSINESS OWNERS ON BUSINESS SUCCESS PRINCIPLES AND TECHNIQUES.

Your pathway to a successful career in business.

$$$$$$$$$$$$$$$$$$$$$$$$$$$$
$$$$$$$$$$$$$$$$$$$$$$$$$$$$
$$$$$$$$$$$$$$$$$$$$$$$$$$$$
$$$$$$$$$$$$$$$$$$$$$$$$$$$$
$$$$$$$$$$$$$$$$$$$$$$$$$$$$
$$$$$$$

COMPILED BY

PHILIP NELSON INSTITUTE OF BUSINESS RESEARCH.

ALL RIGHTS RESERVED.

INTERNATIONAL EDITION.

# A STEP BY STEP GUIDE ON HOW TO START AND GROW A BUSINESS: A PROFESSIONAL TRAINING FOR BUSINESS OWNERS ON BUSINESS SUCCESS PRINCIPLES AND TECHNIQUES.

Hello,

My name is Philip Anochie. I am the President/CEO of Philip Nelson Institute of Business Research. I want to introduce you to a business training manual titled" A step by step guide to how to start and grow a business: Business success principles and techniques.".

This international Business Entrepreneurship Business Training Manual is comprehensive professional business training manual. It is an essential start-up procedure training manual for an individual that wants to start and grow any business.

It is also an invaluable business training manual for all business owners as it revealed the well- guarded secrets of business owners that have started and grown their businesses successfully.

Never miss an opportunity to invest in your future. This manual is your pathway to a successful career in business. It is a catalyst for monumental success in business with compendious topic-by-topic summary notes, solutions and self-assessment questions with answers for business owners and would be business owners.

We have painstakingly compiled a wealth of research experiences in this manual and believe strongly that all business owners will find this manual useful. This manual is a compendium for the mastery of the foundational concepts of business ownership using self-explanatory examples and case studies in business transactions.

Poor performance of businesses in business operations is of international concern. One key threat to explicit comprehension of the workings of businesses is the fact that business has a special methodology to convey its transactions. This manual is comprehensively written in plain language in order to make the subject of business ownership, operations and management simple to understand even to an ordinary beginner in business towards providing a firm foundation in business operations, concepts and principles.

This manual utilizes a topic-by-topic question and answer approach, so as to instill in trainees, well-built problem-solving skills.

The results of our extensive research and experience in business operations are now available. In actuality, this is a complete professional business start-up and operational business training manual that teaches you how to create or improve an existing or functioning business, week by week sequencially.

It enables you to practice key business principles for self –employment such as record keeping, marketing and cash management etc. This business training manual is divided into 12 modules and weekly activities and answers questions such as:

## MODULE 1: WEEK 1: HOW DO I START OR IMPROVE MY BUSINESS?

- How do I start or improve my business?
- How can I manage my finances wisely?
- How do I become a successful business owner?
- How will I improve my business?
- How do I observe a business and think about business success?
- Why do we have to be self –reliant?
- What should I do to improve?
- How will I make daily progress?
- How will I report my progress?

## MODULE 2: WEEK 2: HOW DO I USE THE BUSINESS SUCCESS MAP?

- How do I use the business success map?
- What do people want to buy?
- How do I select the right business?
- How can I learn from business owners?
- How can I learn from customers?
- How do I use market research?

- What should I do to improve?
- How will I make daily progress?
- How will I report my progress?

## MODULE 3: WEEK 3: HOW DO I BUY MY PRODUCT AND SET THE SALES PRICE?

- Did I keep my commitments?
- Would I want this business?
- How can I make profit?
- How do I decrease costs?
- How do I work with suppliers?
- How do I set my price to make profits?
- What should I do to improve?
- How will I make daily progress?
- How will I report my progress?

## MODULE 4: WEEK 4: HOW DO I KNOW IF MY BUSINESS IS MAKING PROFIT?

- Did I keep my commitments?
- How do I know how my business is doing?
- Why should I keep written records?
- How do I develop the habit of keeping records?
- How do I keep an income and expense log?
- What is an income statement?
- How do I create an income and expense log and an income statement?
- What should I do to improve?
- How do I make daily progress?
- How will I report my progress?

## MODULE 5: WEEK 5: HOW DO I SEPARATE MY BUSINESS AND FAMILY MONEY?

- Do I keep my commitments?
- How do I help both my business and my family?

- Why should I separate my business and family money?
- How do I keep separate records?
- How do I separate my money?
- How do I present my business?
- What should I do to improve?
- How will I make daily progress?
- How will I report my progress?

## MODULE 6: WEEK 6: HOW IS MY BUSINESS PROGRESSING?

- Did I keep my commitments?
- How do I describe my business?
- What did I learn?
- Am I becoming more self-reliant?
- What should I do to improve?
- How will I make daily progress?
- How will I report my progress?

## MODULE 7: WEEK 7: HOW WILL I GROW MY BUSINESS?

- Did I keep my commitments?
- What will help my business to make more money?
- How can I make my assets more productive?
- How can I get more productive assets?
- How can I control costs?
- What should I do to improve?
- How will I make daily progress?
- How will I report my progress?

## MODULE 8; WEEK 8: HOW MUCH CAN I AFFORD TO INVEST TO GROW MY BUSINESS?

- Did I keep my commitments?
- Can I afford more assets?
- How much cash is available currently?
- How much cash is available for loan repayments?

- How much cash is available for my business?
- How do I prepare a six-month cash statement of my business?
- What should I do to improve?
- How will I make daily progress?
- How will I report my progress?

## MODULE 9: WEEK 9: HOW DO I KNOW IF I SHOULD USE A LOAN TO GROW MY BUSINESS?

- Did I keep my commitments?
- Is borrowing money good or bad?
- How will the "four rights" help me decide?
- Should I borrow for my business?
- How do I use the loan terms worksheet?
- What should I do to improve?
- How will I make daily progress?
- How will I report my progress?

## MODULE 10: WEEK 10: HOW WIL I ATTRACT MORE CUSTOMERS AND CLOSE SALES?

- Did I keep my commitments?
- Why would customers want to buy from me?
- How will I attract more customers?
- How will I test my marketing plan?
- How will I get customers to buy?
- How will I make it easy to keep buying?
- What should I do to improve ?
- How will I make daily progress?
- How will I report my progress?

## MODULE 11: WEEK 11: HOW WILL I INCREASE MY PROFITS?

- Did I keep my commitments?
- How will I sell more?
- What should I upsell?

- What should my upsell price be?
- How will I upsell?
- How will I sell my products more quickly?
- How will I lower costs?
- What should I do to improve?
- How will I make daily progress?
- How will I report my progress?

## MODULE 12: WEEK 12: HOW DO I CONTINUE TO IMPROVE MY BUSINESS?

- Did I keep my commitments?
- How does everything fit together?
- How will I reach my business goals?
- How do I prepare to graduate from this entrepreneurship training programme?
- What do I do after graduation?
- Am I becoming more self-reliant?
- What should I do to improve?
- How will I make daily progress?
- What do I understand by the Business Success Map?
- How can I continue being self-reliant?
- Am I preparing towards my Certificate in Business Entrepreneurship (CBE)?

*Professional Certificate in Business Entrepreneurship will be issued to all those that bought a copy of this business training manual and correctly answered the questions enclosed at the end of the manual in a written test to be conducted by email.*

Several successful business owners and business executives were interviewed and questioned extensively by our institute to provide a composite to the many proven and profitable business operations to unearth any hidden reasons why they are more successful than the vast majority?

We reveal all their secrets in this manual. Here is your chance to learn the real truth about running a business successfully. If you are looking for ways to run your business profitably, this manual is ideal for you.

Ask me for your own copy of this manual today.

Please contact me for further information in regard to any question you might have.

**Please contact: Philip Nelson Institute of Business Research.**

**Telephone: +2348166582414, +2348140624643, +2348173175179.**

**E-mail:** philipnelsoninstitute@yahoo.com

**A STEP BY STEP GUIDE ON HOW TO START AND GROW A BUSINESS: A PROFESSIONAL TRAINING FOR BUSINESS OWNERS ON BUSINESS SUCCESS PRINCIPLES AND TECHNIQUES.**

Your pathway to a successful career in business.

$$$$$$$$$$$$$$$$$$$$$$$$$$$$

$$$$$$$$$$$$$$$$$$$$$$$$$$$$

$$$$$$$$$$$$$$$$$$$$$$$$$$$$

$$$$$$$$$$$$$$$$$$$$$$$$$$$$

$$$$$$$$$$$$$$$$$$$$$$$$$$$$
$$$$$$$$$$$$$$$$$$$$$$$$$$$$
$$$$

COMPILED BY

PHILIP NELSON INSTITUTE OF BUSINESS RESEARCH.

ALL RIGHTS RESERVED

INTERNATIONAL EDITION

# STARTING AND GROWING MY BUSINESS

### MODULE 1: WEEK 1: HOW DO I START OR IMPROVE MY BUSINESS?

**(A) HOW CAN I MANAGE MY FINANCES WISELY?**
1. Spending less than I earn.
2. Having money in savings.
3. By saving every week.
4. By saving money in a bank.
5. By saving in Banks that offer the best rates for savings.
6. By being free from personal debt.
7. By not taking personal loans more than we are able to pay.
8. By using wisdom in entering business debt.

9. By knowing when a loan can help us grow our business.
10. By protecting myself from financial costs using insurance and government health care programs.
11. By knowing the best insurance provider that is honest.

**(B) HOW WILL I BECOME A SUCCESSFUL BUSINESS OWNER?**

By knowing that what people will like to buy are things that satisfy their need.

( C) HOW WILL I IMPROVE MY BUSINESS

1. By clearly describing my business.
2. By focusing on what makes money and what does not.
3. By getting help from other business owners or leaders.
4. By tracking the progress of my business.

(D) HOW DO I OBSERVE A BUSINESS AND THINK ABOUT BUSINESS SUCCESS?

1. By using the Business Success map shown at the end of this session to observe a business and see if it is following the principles for success.
2. By identifying a business.
3. By asking if the business owner know what people want to buy.
4. By asking if the business owner know how to sell.
5. By asking if the owner knows what people value.
6. By asking if the owner know how to close a sale very well.
7. By finding out if in my business, I do the this successful business owners do.

(E) WHY DOES THE LORD WANT US TO BE SELF-RELIANT?

1. Because he has the power to make us to be self-reliant?
2. Because he will guide us through inspiration.
3. Because he is God of miracles and will make more out of our efforts than we could ever do on our own.

( F) WHAT SHOULD I DO TO IMPROVE?

1. By asking what I can do to start or improve my business this week. I will make it my weekly business goal commitment.
2. By sharing my weekly business goal with others.

( G ) HOW WILL I MAKE DAILY PROGRESS?

1. By choosing an "action partner" that will help us keep our commitments.
2. By contacting my action partner during the week and to report our progress to each other.
3. By making sure that my action partner is of the same gender and are not family members.
4. By deciding when and how we will contact each other.
5. By taking note of my action partner's name and contact information.

Action Partner's Name                           Contact Information

_____                           _____

( H) WHAT ARE MY COMMITMENTS THIS WEEK?

1. I will read each commitment shown below to my action partner and promising to keep my commitments and signing below.
2. I will complete each of the daily Business Success Map activities?
3. I will get a business notebook and bring it to the business meetings.
4. I will achieve my weekly business goal.
5. I will practice how to start and improve my business and teach it to my family.
6. I will add to my savings even a coin or two.
7. I will report to my action partner.
8. I will sign my commitments with my action partner.

My Signature                                   Action Partner's Signature

_____                           _____

( I ) HOW WILL I REPORT MY PROGRESS?

1. I will use a commitment chart to record my progress before the next business meeting.
2. I will record completed daily business success map activities with number of days.
3. I will report that I bought a business notebook.
4. I will report that I achieved my weekly business goal.

5. I will record that I thought the principles to my family.
6. I will report that I added to my savings.
7. I will report my progress to my action partner.
8. I will track my business expenses.

( J ) ACTION AND COMMITMENT

1. I believe in making and keeping my commitments.
2. I build around making commitments and reporting.
3. At the end of each business meeting, I reviewed my actions for the week and add my signature to show commitment.
4. I choose my action partner for the week.
5. The action partner signs my notebook to pledge support.
6. Each day during the week, I contact my action partner to report on my actions and to get help when needed.
7. During the week, I mark my progress in the workbook and use the tools provided, such as work books and other forms.
8. I can call my friends and families if I need extra help.
9. At the beginning of the next business, I will return and report on my commitments.
10. I will make it a comfortable, powerful experience for everyone.
11. I will think about how people are helped by making commitments and reporting.

( K ) HOW DO I USE THE SUCCESS MAP?

1. Every day this week, I will observe, reflect and ponder on the principles of business success.
2. I will visit businesses for one or two hours each day to observe them.
3. I will take my business notebook and business success map when I visit local businesses.
4. My daily activities using the business success map will be as shown below:

DAILY ACTIVITIES

DAY 1: CUSTOMERS

Watch what, when and how much customers buy. Review the customer principles shown on the map. Record your thoughts.

DAY 2: SALES

How do businesses sell their products or services? Review the sales principles shown on the map. Record your thoughts.

DAY 3: COSTS

Think about the costs the businesses have. How do they reduce costs? Review the cost principles shown on the map. Record your thoughts.

DAY 4: PROFIT

Did the businesses keep track of their income and costs? If it were your business, how would you track your money? Review the profits principles shown on the map. Record your thoughts.

REPEAT ON DAY 5: CUSTOMER AND SALES.

REPEAT ON DAY 6: PROFITS AND COSTS.

BUSINESS SUCCESS MAP: The principles of business success.

   (A)   BUSINESS SUCCESS: How do I run my business?
1. Separate personal and business records.
2. Keep daily records.
3. Pay tithing first.
4. Save weekly.
5. Improve something every day.
6. Learn continually.
7. Use the foundational principles.
8. Set exciting measurable goals.
9. Start small. Think Big.
10. Never give up.

( B) CUSTOMERS: WHY DO PEOPLE WANT TO BUY?

1. Know why people buy your product.
2. Know what customers value.
3. Learn from customers daily.

( C) SALES: HOW DO I SELL?

1. Always upsell
2. Turn inventory often.
3. Ask, listen, suggest.
4. Make it easy to buy.
5. Close the sale.

( D ) PROFIT: HOW DO I INCREASE PROFITS?

1. Keep daily records.
2. Pay yourself a salary.
3. Seek daily profit.
4. Buy low. Sell high.
5. Don't steal from your business.
6. Use productive assets.

( E ) COSTS: HOW CAN I CONTROL MY COSTS?

1. Lower costs.
2. Use multiple suppliers.
3. Only add fixed costs when they can increase profits.
4. Make investments wisely.
5. Use the four rights to borrow wisely.

MODULE 2: WHAT DO PEOPLE WANT TO BUY?

(A ) DID I KEEP MY COMMITMENTS?

1. I must complete the daily business map activities which will help my business.
2. I must work on my weekly business goal.

3. I will write what I learnt from keeping my commitments in my business notebook.

( B ) WHAT DO PEOPLE WANT TO BUY?

1. I will talk to business owners and customers and choose a product or service that solves customer's problems.
2. I will select the right business with products that customers will want to buy.
3. I will select the right business that I can provide my skills, interests and experience.
4. I will select the right business that will be a good business for me.
5. I will select the right business that will increase my income and provide me with adequate revenues and profits.
6. I will select the right business that will give me "ease of entry", low competition, suppliers and capital.

( C ) HOW DO I SELECT THE RIGHT BUSINESS?

1. I will consider a type of business.
2. I will write one or two businesses that interests me.
3. I will identify the specific customer needs in the business category that interests me.
4. I will see in the business what customers will like to buy.
5. I will identify the needs my business will like to meet.
6. The business is what I am good at and interested in doing.
7. I can start the business easily.
8. I can grow and change the business to be more profitable.
9. The money, competition and suppliers needed is low.
10. The business will help me to increase my income and make me become more reliant.
11. I have identified where I can make profit in the business.
12. The business I want to learn about is _____

( D ) HOW CAN I LEARN FROM BUSINESS OWNERS?

1. I now have some idea about my business?
2. I am going to do market research to test my idea and learn more.

3. I will watch people, talk with customers, talk with competitors, and try products.
4. I will find real needs and answers.
5. I will practice the questions that I will ask business owners this week.
6. I will explain to people my own business or the type of business I wish to start.
7. I will introduce myself and ask the questions below, give feedback and try again.

INTRODUCTION: Hello, I'm------------------(Name) .And you? I'm in business class and we're trying to learn how businesses succeed. May I ask some questions?

CUSTOMER NEEDS AND PRODUCT.

1. What do your customers buy most?
2. Why do you think your customers buy what you sell?
3. Who are your competitors?
4. What makes your business better than theirs?

SUPPLIERS AND PROFIT

1. Where do you get your product?
2. Are there other suppliers?
3. Do you think you could find a lower cost if you buy more at a time?
4. What is your price?
5. How did you decide on the price?
6. Are you profitable?
7. What would happen if you raised or lowered your price?

SALES

1. About how many can you sell each day?
2. How do you find new customers?
3. How important is your location?
4. What have been some keys to your success?
5. What have been your biggest problems?

Every day this week, I will talk to business owners and write what I learn in my business notebook. I will write the questions that I will ask business owners.

( E ) HOW CAN I LEARN FROM CUSTOMERS.

1. I will learn from customers daily to become a successful business owner.
2. I can learn a lot by observing my customers and talking with them.
3. Customers can make or break my business.
4. I must listen and learn from my customers.
5. I will practice the questions that I will ask customers this week with somebody.
6. I will imagine that the person is my customer.
7. I will ask the question below as they relate to my business or business idea.
8. I will take notes, switch roles, give each other helpful feedback and practice any weakness.

INTRODUCTION: Hello, I'm _____(Name). And you? I'm in a business class and we're learning about customers. May I ask a few questions?

CUSTOMER NEEDS AND PRODUCT

1. What do you buy from this business?
2. If you could, what would you change about the product?
3. If you could, what would you change about the business?
4. Have you bought this product at other places?
5. Were they better or worse? Why?

SALES AND PROFIT

1. What do you like about buying this product here?
2. What would make you want to buy more?
3. Is the price about right?
4. Would you buy more at a lower price?
5. Would you still buy as much if they raised the price?
6. Is the location important?

OBSERVATIONS: Watch customers to find answers. Do not ask the following questions.

1. Are they mostly women or men or a mixture?
2. Are they younger or older?
3. Do they seem to have more money or less money?
4. What time of the day do they buy?
5. How much do they buy?

Every day this week, I will talk to my customers and write what I learn in my business notebook.

1. I will write the questions that I will ask customers this week in my business notebook.
2. I will write my thoughts in my business notebook.

( F ) HOW DO I USE MARKET RESEARCH

1. Once I have done market research, I will need to evaluate what I have learnt.
2. I will practice the evaluation process.
3. I will choose somebody to work with me.
4. I will look at the profits, competition, and suppliers of two businesses.

BUSINESS A EVALUATION.

| PIECES SOLD (Daily average) | 200 | UNITS PER MONTH | EVALUATION 5000 |
|---|---|---|---|
| Selling price | 5 per piece (average) | Units per month | 25,000 |
| Cost to buy | 4 per piece (average) | Costs per month) | 20, 200 |
| Competition | 6 businesses | Profit | 4, 800 |
| Suppliers | 2 Suppliers, distant | | |

BUSINESS B EVALUATION

| ITEMS SOLD (Daily average) | 20 | Units per month | 500 |
|---|---|---|---|
| Selling price | 100 per item (Average). | Sales per month | 50,000 |
| Cost to buy | 80 per item (Average) | Costs per month | 40,000 |

| Competition | None nearby | Profit | 10,000 |
| Suppliers | 3 suppliers nearby. | | |

5. Which business would you choose?
6. Why would you choose the business?
7. What other questions would you ask about these businesses or their customers?
8. I will prepare to decide on my business this week.
9. During the week, I will review all I have learnt and come to the next business meeting with a business idea. (either a new business or improved business).
10. If I already have a business, I will decide if it is the best option for me.
11. If I already have a business, I will decide if it is the best option for me.

( G ) WHAT SHOULD I DO TO IMPROVE?

1. I will find the idea that will help my business the most this week.
2. I will make this idea my weekly business goal.
3. I will add my weekly business goal to my commitments next week.
4. I will share my weekly business goal with others.

( H ) HOW WILL I MAKE DAILY PROGRESS?

1. I will commit myself by choosing an action partner.
2. I will decide when and how I will contact my action partner.
3. I will record my action partner's name and contact information
4. I will read each commitment aloud to my action partner.
5. I will promise to keep my commitments by signing my signature below.
6. I will observe and interview at least 10 business owners and customers to understand what people want to buy.
7. I will choose a new business or decide how to improve my business.
8. I will achieve my weekly business goal.
9. I will practice what I have learnt and teach it to my family.
10. I will add to my savings- even a coin or two.
11. I will report to my action partner.

My Signature                                   Action Partner's Signature

_____                            _____

(I) HOW WILL I REPORT MY PROGRESS?

1. Before the next meeting, I will use a commitment chart to record my progress.
2. I will record the number of times I kept the commitment.
3. I will observe and interview at least 10 business owners and customers.
4. I will choose a new business or way to improve my business.
5. I will achieve my weekly business goal.
6. I will practice the business principles learnt and teach it to my family.
7. I will add to my savings.
8. I will report to my action partner.
9. I will track my personal expenses.

SUMMARY: WHAT PEOPLE BUY.

A successful business is all about helping people solve their problems. It is about understanding customers. If someone has a need and you help them solve it, they will PAY you. And that's good! But how do you find out what customers need? What do people want to buy?

SELECTING THE RIGHT BUSINESS

How will you choose the right business for you? Or, if you have a business, how do you know if it is the right one. Here are four key questions that will help you make the best decision.

1. What do people buy?
2. What do people buy that I could provide?
3. What do people buy that I could provide, that is a business I could start preety easily and
4. That will increase my income and help me become self-reliant? Or in other words, I need to make my decision based on:
   1. Customers and products.

2. My own skills, interests and experience.
3. The environment, including competition, suppliers and money, and
4. The potential for revenues and profits.

( J ) LEARN ABOUT SIMILAR BUSINESSES

1. I will visit and watch businesses like the one I might start (my competitors)
2. I will keep my commitments.
3. I will find out what is working for them.
4. I will find out what is not working well for them.
5. I will talk to people who run the businesses.
6. In order to avoid feelings of competitiveness, I will talk with people outside my area.
7. I will use the questions listed below.
8. I will add other questions.
9. I will make it a conversation.
10. I will be sure to show gratitude.
11. I will do this every day this week (except Sunday).
12. I will record my answers and the things I learn in my notebook.

INTRODUCTION: Hello, I'm -------------(Name). And you? . I'm in a business class and we're trying to learn how businesses succeed. May I ask some questions?

CUSTOMER NEEDS , PRODUCTS

1. What do customers buy most?
2. Why do you think your customers buy what you sell?
3. Who are your competitors?
4. What is unique about your business?

SUPPLIERS, PROFIT

1. Where do you get your products? Are there other suppliers?
2. Do you think you could find a lower cost if you buy more at a time?
3. What is your price? How did you decide on this price? Are you profitable?
4. What would happen if you raised or lowered your price?

SALES

1. About how many can you sell each day?
2. How do you find new customers?
3. How important is your location?
4. What have been some keys to your success?
5. What are your biggest headaches?

(K) LEARN ABOUT SIMILAR CUSTOMERS.

1. I will talk to people who are customers of businesses like the one I may start. I will watch them and learn all that I can.
2. I will do this every day this week (except Sunday).
3. I will record their answers and the things I learn in my notebook.
4. I will use the questions listed below.
5. I will add other questions.
6. I will make it a conversation.
7. I will be sure to show my gratitude.

INTRODUCTION: Hello, I'm ------------(Name). And you? I'm in a business class and we're learning about customers. May I ask a few questions?

CUSTOMER NEEDS, PRODUCT.

1. What do you buy from this business?
2. If you could, what would you change about this product? About the business?
3. Have you bought this product at other places? Were they better or worse? Why?

SALES, PROFIT

1. What do you like about buying this product here?
2. What would make you to buy more?
3. Is the price about right? Would you buy more at a lower price?
4. Would you still buy as much if they raised the price?
5. Is the location important?

OBSERVATIONS: Do not ask the following questions: Watch customers to find answers.

1. Are they mostly women or men or a mixture?
2. Are they younger or older?
3. Do they seem to have more money or less money?
4. What time of the day do they buy?
5. How much do they buy?

MODULE 3: WEEK 3: HOW DO I BUY MY PRODUCT AND SET THE SALES PRICE?

( A ) DID I KEEP MY COMMITMENTS?

1. I will report my commitments.
2. I will report what I learnt as I observed and interviewed business owners and customers.
3. I will find out how the information obtained will help my business.
4. If I have not chosen a business, yet, I will have an idea for a business.
5. If I have chosen a business, I will name the business that I have chosen.
6. If I already have a business, I will choose improvements for my business.
7. I will list the improvements that I have chosen in my notebook.
8. I will write what I have learnt working on my weekly business goal.
9. I will write in my notebook what I have learnt by keeping my commitments.

( B ) WOULD I WANT THIS BUSINESS?

1. I will know how to buy my product and set the sales price.
2. I will find a source for my product and choose a price.
3. I will learn and practice skills that will help me buy my product and set the sales price.
4. During this next week, I will learn how to talk with suppliers to " buy low", or buy at a low price.

5. I will also learn how to set a price in order to "sell high"- that is, make a profit.
6. I will read the costs and sales section of the Business Success Map.

(C) HOW CAN I MAKE PROFIT?

1. I need to start making money in my business.
2. Sales price minus purchase price equals to profit.
3. I will make profit if I lower the purchase price (the price I pay the supplier).
4. I will make profit if I raise the sales price (the price I charge the customer). We do not have unlimited control over sales price or our costs. We do have some control. Successful business owners try to increase the sales price and decrease the purchase price. Successful business owners buy low and sell high.
5. I know that businesses make profit.
6. Another reason to buy low and sell high is that all businesses have more expenses than just the cost of the product like transportation and wages.
7. By buying low and selling high, business owners are able to cover costs, pay themselves wages, and still make a little profit. This is starting to be a real business.
8. I will find out what I can do to control costs and make my business to be more profitable.

(D) HOW DO I DECREASE COSTS?

1. I will close my business if I do not decrease costs.
2. I will decrease costs by having many suppliers and chose the low cost one among them.

(E) HOW DO I WORK WITH SUPPLIERS?

1. It is crucial for me to talk to my suppliers.
2. This week, I will speak with people who can supply me with their product or my product ingredients.
3. I will speak to people who will help me provide my service.
4. I will write what I have learnt in my business notebook.

5. With my action partner, I will practice the questions I will ask suppliers this week.
6. I will explain to my partner, the kind of supplier I need to talk to for my business.
7. I will take turns asking the questions and giving helpful feedback.
8. I will take notes in my business notebook.
9. I will ask specific questions that will help me to improve my business.

INTRODUCTION: Hello, I'm ----------(Name) . And you? I'm thinking about starting a business where I would need the products you supply. May I ask a few questions?

PRODUCT

1. What products sell best for you?
2. Why do you think business owners buy what you supply?
3. How do you check for quality? (Try to observe quality).
4. How much can you supply ? Do you have production limits?

PRICE

1. How much do you charge? Do you offer any discounts?
2. How do you decide on these prices?
3. What do you think will happen, if you changed prices?

SALES, COMPETITION

1. Do you help your buyers sell the product?
2. Who buys the most of your product?
3. Why are they successful?
4. Who are your competitors?
5. What is unique about them?

I will add any other questions I have. I will be sure I thank them and write down what I have learnt in my business notebook.

I will practice at least once and discuss together with my partner. I will speak with suppliers this week. I will find out if I have other questions to ask them.

I will write my thoughts in my business notebook.

( E ) HOW DO I SET MY PRICE TO MAKE A PROFIT?

1. Every business has to earn more than it spends.
2. I know how I will talk to suppliers to find quality products at low cost, or buy low.
3. I will find out how I will set the price, or sell high.
4. I will find out the best cost I can get from suppliers.
5. I will find out other costs I have (Utilities, supplies, rent etc.).
6. I will find out the wages I need to pay myself and others.
7. I will find out how I can add value and make my product different.
8. I know that convenience, service, friendliness and quality can all add value and make me different.
9. What do competitors charge?
10. Can I charge more based on added value?
11. Given all these factors, I will know how much profit I can make so that my business can grow and succeed. More is good.

How much do you buy your product = 5 per item

Wages, transportation and delivery costs = 2 per item.

Competitors sell to customers for 8 -10 per item.

You need to make as much profit as possible after adding value to your product= 7 per item.

12. What price did you decide to set for your product and why?
13. How could you discover how much customers are willing to pay?
14. How can you control costs, add value, and set the right price so that your business can make a profit?

(F)   WHAT SHOULD I DO TO IMPROVE?

1. I will ponder on what I have learnt and record it in my notebook.
2. I will find the idea that will help my business the most this week.
3. I will make the idea my weekly business goal.
4. I will add the weekly business goal to my commitments.
5. I will share my weekly business goal with others.

(G) HOW WILL I MAKE DAILY PROGRESS?
1. I will choose my action partner.
2. I will decide where and how we will contact each other.
3. I will take my action partner's name and contact information.
4. I will read each commitment aloud to my action partner.
5. I will promise to keep my commitments by signing my signature.
6. I will interview at least 4 suppliers and find sources for my product.
7. I will write the number of suppliers that I will interview.
8. I will set my initial selling price.
9. I will achieve my weekly business goal.
10. I will practice today's business principle and teach it to my family.
11. I will add to my savings even a coin or two.
12. I will report to my action partner.
13. I will sign my commitments with my action partner.

(H) HOW WILL I REPORT MY PROGRESS?
1. Before the next meeting, I will use a commitment chart to record my progress.
2. I will record the number of times I kept my commitment.
3. I will interview at least 4 suppliers.
4. I will set my initial selling price.
5. I will practice the business principle learnt and teach it to my family.
6. I will add to my savings – even a coin or two.
7. I will report to my action partner.
8. I will track my personal expenses.

If you buy for a dollar and sell for a dollar, you will not make any profit.


WEEK FOUR: HOW DO I KNOW IF MY BUSINESS IS MAKING PROFIT?

(A) DID I KEEP MY COMMITMENTS?
1. I will keep my commitments.
2. I will learn from the interviewed suppliers to find the best prices and sources (to buy low).
3. I will find out how it will help my business.

4. I will learn as I set my initial selling price (to sell high).
5. I will find out how it will help my business.
6. I will record all I have learnt by working on my weekly business goal.
7. I will write what I have learnt from keeping my commitments in my business notebook.

(B) HOW DO I KNOW HOW MY BUSINESS IS DOING?
(1) I will find out if my business is profitable through the records in my business notebook.
(2) I will find out if all my customers have paid me through my records.
(3) I will know my total expenses through my records.
(4) I will track all income and expenses on a log everyday from now on to know if my business is making a profit.
(5) I will learn skills that will help me answer questions and perform actions.
(6) I will read the profit section of the Business Success Map.

(C) WHY SHOULD I KEEP WRITTEN RECORDS?
1. I will study Daniel's furniture business with a partner.
2. I will find out how much the business spends this week.
3. I will find out how much the business takes in this week.
4. I will find out how much profit or loss the business have this week.
5. I cannot remember all the income, expenses and profit without looking at written records.

(C) HOW DO I DEVELOP THE HABIT OF KEEPING RECORDS.
1. I know that successful business owners keep records.
2. I should enjoy keeping records.
3. It should be a habit for me.
4. Nothing should prevent me from keeping records.
5. I should know why I am keeping records.
6. I know the people that will benefit from my record keeping such as my children.
7. I should develop skills on record keeping.
8. I know that I may need new skills to be good at keeping records.
9. I will choose friends not accomplices.
10. I know that friends help me to do the right thing.
11. I know that accomplices help me to do the wrong thing.

12. I will ask those around me including my spouse to help me in keeping records.
13. I know that my business training will help me to learn these skills.
14. I will use rewards and penalties wisely and sparingly.
15. I will reward myself for keeping daily records.
16. I will get the tools because I cannot dig a well without a tool.
17. I will make sure I have the tools to do what needs to be done.
18. I know the tools I will use to keep records.
19. I will learn about some tools in this training manual.
20. The tools for keeping records are copies of income and expense log, income statement, ledger book and notebook at point of sale.

( E) HOW DO I KEEP AN INCOME AND EXPENSE LOG

1. I know that an income and expense log is a common business form.
2. We should use it every day to record the money coming in and the money going out of our businesses. Daniel started keeping track of his income and expenses by using the following steps:

Daniel started keeping track of his income and expenses by matching the numbers below to the income and expense log book as shown below:

STEPS TO CREATE AN INCOME AND EXPENSE LOG

1. Daniel has 1500 in his business cash box. He put that amount as his starting balance at the beginning of the week.
   MONDAY
2. Sold 4 chairs . In the income column, he puts 200.
3. Adds 200 to the cash balance. New balance= 1700.
4. Paid 100 in rent. In the expense column, he puts 100.
5. Subtracts 100 from the cash balance . New balance= 1600.
   TUESDAY
6. Paid 500 to Maxwell . In the expense column, he puts 500.
7. Subtracts 500 from the cash balance . New balance=1100
   WEDNESDAY
8. Sold a table and a chair set. In the income column, he puts 400.
9. Adds 400 to the cash balance. New balance =1500.

THURSDAY

10. Sold bedroom furniture. In the income column, he puts 1000.
11. Add 1000 to the cash balance. New balance =2500.

FRIDAY

12. Bought materials. In the expense column, he puts 1,500.
13. Subtracts 1500 from the cash balance. New balance = 1000.

SATURDAY

14. Sold a table. In the income column, he puts 400.
15. Adds 400 to the cash balance. New balance =1400.
16. Daniel finishes the week with 1400 in his business cash box.

Daniel wrote down his income and expenses every day. His income and expense log looked like this at the end of the week.

DANIEL'S FURNITURE INCOME AND EXPENSE LOG: AUGUST 14$^{th}$ TO 20$^{th}$ AUGUST. DANIEL'S BUSINESS STARTING BALANCE= 1500 (1).

| DATE | DESCRIPTION | EXPENSE | INCOME | CASH BALANCE |
|---|---|---|---|---|
| MON 14/5 | Sold 4 chairs | | 200 (2) | 1700 (3) |
| MON 15/5 | Paid rent | - 100 (4) | | 1600 (5) |
| TUE 16/5 | Paid wages to Maxwell | -500 (6) | | 1100 (7) |
| WED 17/5 | Sold a table and chair set | | 400 (8) | 1500 (9) |
| THUR 18/5 | Sold bedroom furniture | | 1000 (10) | 2500 (11) |
| FRI 19/5 | Paid for materials | -500 (12) | | 1000 (13) |
| SAT 20/5 | Sold a table | | 400 (14) | 1400 (15) |
| | | | | 1400 (16) |

Daniel's employee, Maxwell, said he had not been paid. How does this log help Daniel resolve that issue?

(F) WHAT IS AN INCOME STATEMENT?

1. Another important business form is the income statement.

2. It is hard to calculate profit from memory.
3. An income statement will help.
4. An income statement will summarize all transactions during a period such as a week, month, quarter, or year.
5. The summary tells us whether the business is profitable during that period.
6. An income statement shows income , expenses , profit or loss.
7. I will match the numbers below in the income statement on the following page.

STEPS TO CREAT AN INCOME STATEMENT.

INCOME:

1. For total sales of chairs, he puts 200.
2. For total sales of tables, he puts 400.
3. For total sales of dinning room sets, he puts 400.
4. For total sales of bedroom sets, he puts 1000.
5. He adds his total sales. His total income for the week: 2000.

EXPENSES

6. For the cost of rent, he puts 100.
7. For the cost of materials , he puts 1500.
8. For employee wages , he puts 500.
9. He adds his total expenses. Total expenses for the week 2100.

PROFIT ( OR LOSS)

10. He subtracts his expenses from his income. 2000- 2100= 100.
11. I understand what this income statement tells me about Daniel's business.
12. I understand the period covered by this income statement .
13. I understand whether or not Daniel's business was profitable this week.
14. I understand why or why not Daniel will operate this business this week.

Successful business owners seek daily profit.

DANIEL'S FURNITURE BUSINESS INCOME STATEMENT.

MONDAY- SATURDAY INCOME

Sales of chairs 200 (1)

Sales of table 400 (2)

Sales of dining room set 400 (3).

Sales of bedroom set 1000 (4)

---

Total income       2000   (5)

EXPENSES

Rent              100 ( 6 )

Materials         1500

Employee wage     500

---

Total expenses    2100 ( 10 )

Profit ( or loss) 100 (10 )

( G) HOW DI I CREATE AN INCOME AND EXPENSE LOG AND AN INCOME STATEMENT.

1. To know if our business is profitable , we need an income statement.
2. To create an income statement , we need the income and expense log.
3. I have seen how Daniel kept an income and expense log and how he used that to make an income statement .
4. I will work with a partner to make an income statement for Joseph.
5. I will complete the income and expense log and the income statement below.
6. I will create an income expense log for Joseph's construction business.
7. I will create an income statement for Joseph's construction business.
8. If I need help creating the income and expense log or the income statement , I will turn to the answer key below.

MONDAY: Collected 50% down payment on a job : 2000.

TUESDAY: Paid 1500 for materials. WEDNESDAY: Worked on the job.

THURSDAY: Worked on the job. FRIDAY: Paid another 1000 for materials.

SATURDAY: Finished the job. Paid an employee: 500, collected remaining 2000.

9. I learn about Joseph's business from seeing his income statement.
10. Small business owners everywhere rely on the power of these forms.
11. Keeping income and expense logs or income statements help.
12. To start keeping records, I will copy the income and expense log and the income statement into my business notebook.
13. I will record my income and expenses everyday, and at the end of the week, create an income statement.
14. I will continue to do this every day and week as my business grows.
15. I will need these business records for the group meetings in weeks seven and eight.
16. I will learn how keeping records helped Vangeli's street magician grow his business.

INCOME AND EXPENSE LOG: MONDAY TO SATURDAY

| DATE | DESCRIPTION: BUSINESS STARTING | EXPENSE | INCOME BALANCE | BALANCE |
|---|---|---|---|---|
| 21 | Down payment | | (1) 2000 | 3000 |
| 22 | Materials | (2) -1500 | | 5000 |
| 25 | Paid employee | (3) -1000 | | 3500 |
| 26 | Final payment | (4) -500 | | 2500 |
| | | | | 2000 |
| | | | (5) 2000 | 4000 |
| | TOTAL EXPENSES AND INCOME | | | 4000 |

17. Joseph calculates his new balance as he adds each new entry on the log.
1. On Monday, Joseph calculated a down payment, so that goes in the income column.
2. For Tuesday, the amount Joseph paid for materials goes in the expense column.

3. For Wednesday and Thursday, Joseph worked on the job.
4. For Friday, the amount Joseph paid for more materials goes in the expense column. The amount collected for finishing the job goes in the income column.

JOSEPH'S CONSTRUCTION BUSINESS: INCOME STATEMENT : MONDAY TO SATURDAY.

INCOME: DOWN PAYMENT: 2000 ; FINAL PAYMENT: 2000 ;

TOTAL INCOME = 4000

EXPENSES : MATERIALS; 2500; EMPLOYEE WAGE: 500. TOTAL EXPENSES: 3000. PROFIT (OR LOSS)= 1000.

At the end of the job, Joseph transfers the amount to an income statement to see how much he made on the job.

( H ) WHAT SHOULD I IMPROVE ?

1. I will quietly ponder what I am learning.
2. I will write my impressions in my business notebook.
3. I will find the idea that helps my business the most this week.
4. I will make the idea my weekly business goal.
5. I will add my weekly business goal to my commitments.
6. I will share my weekly business goal and other impressions.

( I ) HOW DO I MAKE DAILY PROGRESS?

1. I will set the time 10 minutes for this commitment section.
2. I will choose an action partner.
3. I will decide when and how I will contact my action partner.
4. I will note my action partner's name and contact information.
5. I will read each commitment aloud to my action partner.
6. I will promise to keep my commitments by signing my signature below.
7. I will keep my commitments.

MY COMMITMENTS

1. I will use an income and expense log everyday.

2. I will create a business income statement at the end of the week.
3. I will achieve my weekly business goal.
4. I will practice today's activity and teach it to my family.
5. I will add to my savings – even a coin or two.
6. I will report to my action partner.

_____        _____

My signature                                                     My action partner's signature

( J ) HOW WILL I REPORT MY PROGRESS

1. I will record my progress and the number of times I kept the commitment.
2. I used an income and expense log every day for 7 days.
3. I create an income statement.
4. I achieved my weekly business goals .
5. I practiced the business principles I learnt and thought them to my family.
6. I added to my savings.
7. I reported to my action partner.
8. I will track my personal expenses.

WEEK FIVE: HOW DO I SEPARATE MY BUSINESS AND FAMILY MONEY?

(A ) DID I KEEP MY COMMITMENTS

1. I will report my commitments.
2. I will learn as I kept an income and expense log about my business.
3. I will find out how what I have learnt will help my business.
4. I will write what I learnt by creating a business income statement.
5. I will find out how what I have learnt will help my business.
6. I will note what I have learnt by working on my weekly business goal.

(B)   HOW DO I HELP BOTH MY BUSINESS AND MY FAMILY?

1. I have started to keep records of my business money as it comes in and out.
2. I will read the business section of the business success map.
3. I will keep separate  accounts and daily records for my business and family money , and I will pay myself a wage.

( C) WHY SHOULD I SEPARATE MY BUSINESS AND FAMILY MONEY?

1. It is important to separate business and personal money and to pay ourself a wage.
2. A business owner is both an owner and an employee.
3. We know that great blessing come from paying tithing on our income. If we keep our business money and our personal money separate , it is easier to calculate our tithing.
4. I will keep business and personal money in separate accounts or locations.
5. I pay tithing on personal income (salary or commission) that we get from the business.
6. Money in the business is not tithed.
7. The money in the business is used to pay for business expenses, wages and growth.
8. If friends and family needs money, successful business owners don't steal from their from their business.
9. Successful business owners pay tithing first.

( D ) HOW DO I KEEP SEPARATE RECORDS?

1. We keep separate records to separate business and personal money.
2. I keep daily records of all the money that comes to my business and all that goes out.
3. I keep daily records of all the money that comes to my family and all that goes out.
4. The records are called " income and expense logs".
5. I keep two separate logs – one for business money and one for personal money.
6. Lenders will often want to see a business income and expense log before making a loan.
7. Keeping careful records will help me to be more ready if I decide to borrow to grow my business.

Look at this sample of Maria's business income and expense log. Notice that on August 16 (the day Maria's brother asked her for money), Maria's business had 3200 in the bank account.

MARIA (BUSINESS) INCOME AND EXPENSE LOG : AUGUST 14- 20.

| DATE : | DESCRIPTION | EXPENSE | INCOME | MARIA'S BUSINESS CASH BALANCE = 2600. |
|---|---|---|---|---|
| August 14 | Purchased feed | -300 | | 2300 |
| August 15 | Egg sales | | 500 | 2800 |
| August 16 | Egg sales | | 400 | 3200 |
| August 17 | Maria's wage | (-3000) | | 200 |
| August 18 | Egg sales | | 600 | 800 |
| August 19 | Purchased feed | -600 | | 200 |
| August 20 | Egg sales | | 700 | 900 |

8. Maria would not be able to pay herself her 3000 wage the next day if she gives her brother 1000.
9. Maria's wage is an expense to the business and an income to her personal money.
10. Maria is correct to pay her tithing on her personal income.

MARIA'S ( PERSONAL) INCOME AND EXPENSE LOG: August 14- 20.

| DATE | DESCRIPTION | EXPENSE | INCOME | CASH BALANCE: MARIA'S (PERSONAL) CASH BALANCE = 600. |
|---|---|---|---|---|
| Aug 14 | Food | -100 | | 500 |
| Aug 15 | Clothing | -200 | | 300 |
| Aug 16 | Bus pass | -200 | | 100 |
| Aug 17 | Wage | | (3000) | 3100 |
| Aug 18 | Tithing | -300 | | 2800 |
| Aug 19 | Food | -1500 | | 1300 |
| Aug 20 | Rent | -600 | | 700 |

WAGES OR COMMISSION?

If there is not enough cash in Maria's business to pay her a regular wage, she can pay herself a commission based on sales. Successful business owners keep daily records.

( E ) HOW DO I SEPARATE MY MONEY?
1. I will practice separating my business and personal money.
2. I will look at the personal income and expenses for each day of the week.
3. I will record my business money in my business income and expense log.
4. I will record my personal money in my personal income and expense log.
5. I will create my personal income statement from the information in my personal log.
6. I will create my personal income statement from the information in my personal log.
7. I will learn from this exercise.
8. If I make mistake, I will understand why.
9. If I understand, I can help those who are confused.
10. Successful business owners keep daily records and use them to make wise business decisions.

While Maria does not enjoy keeping records, she makes herself keep separate records for her business and personal money every day. This is a smart way to do business. Plus she also knows that if she ever needs a business loan, lenders will want to see daily records.

See how Daniel improved his business by using the principles of record keeping. Successful business owners separate their business and personal records.

Monday 2/9 sold 100 bottles at 10 each. Bought food for family for 300.

Tuesday 3/9 Paid 800 for business supplies. Sold 30 bottles at 10 each.

Wednesday 4/9 Paid 500 for kids school fees. Paid yourself a wage of 1000. Paid 100 for tithing.

Thursday 5/9 Paid 500 for personal rent. Sold 10 ice blocks at 10 each.

Friday 6/9 Sold 100 bottles at 10 each. Paid business fees of 200.

Saturday 7/9 Sold 20 bottles at 10 each. Bought new clothes for 100.

MY BUSINESS INCOME AND EXPENSES 2/9 – 7/9

| DATE | DESCRIPTION | EXPENSE | INCOME | BALANCE: BUSINESS CASH BALANCE = 1000 |
|---|---|---|---|---|
| 2/9 | Sold 100 bottles (1) | | 1000 | 2000 |
| 3/9 | Business supplies (3) | -800 | | 1200 |
| 3/9 | Sold 30 bottles (4) | | 300 | 1500 |
| 4/9 | Wages (6) | -1000 | | 500 |
| 5/9 | Sold 10 ice blocks (9) | | 100 | 600 |
| 6/9 | Sold 100 bottles (10) | | 1000 | 1600 |
| 6/9 | Business fees (11) | -200 | | 1400 |
| 7/9 | Sold 20 bottles (12) | | 200 | 1600 |
| Total expenses and income | | 2000 | 2600 | 1600 |

MY PERSONAL INCOME AND EXPENSES 2/9 – 7/9

| DATE | DESCRIPTION | EXPENSE | INCOME | BALANCE: PERSONAL CASH BALANCE 1000 |
|---|---|---|---|---|
| 2/9 | Food (2) | -300 | | 1000 |
| 4/9 | School fees (5) | -500 | | 700 |
| 4/9 | Wage (6) | | 1000 | 200 |
| 4/9 | Tithing (7) | -100 | | 1200 |

| 5/9 | Rent (8) | -500 | | 1100 |
|---|---|---|---|---|
| 7/9 | Shirt (13) | -100 | | 600 |
| | | | | 500 |
| Total expense and income | | 1500 | 1000 | 500 |

1. I have learnt important skills today that will help me to succeed.
2. I will work hard this week to make these skills a habit.
3. I will keep separate accounts and daily records.

MY BUSINESS INCOME STATEMENT ( 2/9- 7/9)

INCOME  (1) (4) (10) (12)

Sales of water bottles           2500

Sales of ice blocks (9)           100

Total business income           2600

EXPENSES

Supplies ( 3)           800

Business fees (11)           200

Wages ( 6 )           1000

Total Business Expenses    2000

Business profit (or loss) (income- expenses) = 600

MY PERSONAL INCOME STATEMENT (2/9 – 7/9)

INCOME

Wage (6 )           1000

Total personal income    1000

EXPENSES

| | |
|---|---|
| Tithing (7) | 100 |
| Rent (8) | 500 |
| Food (2) | 300 |
| Other (5) (13) | 600 |
| Total personal expenses | 1500 |

Personal profit (or loss)  (Income – Expenses ) = 500.

(4) I will find out who and what might make it hard for me to keep separate records.

(5) I can make a plan to make it easier.

(6) I can do it at same time each day.

(7) I can keep records in a specific place.

(8) I can create reminders for myself.

(9) I can write my plan.

(F) HOW DO I PRESENT MY BUSINESS?

1. I can make a presentation about my business.
2. I an able to describe my business to others.
3. I want to hear suggestions about my business.
4. I can present in a way most comfortable to me.

MY BUSINESS IN THREE MINUTES- INSTRUCTIONS.

PART ONE : In less than one minute, describe your business.

PART TWO: In less than one minute, describe how answering one of the following questions greatly improved your business.

1. What do people want to buy?
2. How do I sell?
3. How do I control costs?

4. How do I increase profits?
   5. How do I run my business?

PART THREE: In less than one minute, describe one thing you will do to continue improving your business.

   1. This week I will think about what I will share.
   2. I will describe my business in a business notebook.
   3. I will practice giving presentations to my family and friends.
   4. I will share my business presentation with others.
   5. I will find an idea that will help my business the most this week.
   6. I will make the idea my weekly business goal.

(G) HOW WILL I MAKE DAILY PROGRESS?

   1. I will choose my action partner.
   2. I will decide when and how we will contact each other.
   3. I will record my action partner's name and contact information.
   4. I will read my commitment aloud to my action partner.
   5. I will promise to keep my commitments by signing my signature below.
   6. I will keep separate records for business and personal money.
   7. I will pay myself a wage or commission regularly and keep that personal money in a separate location or account from my business money.
   8. I will prepare a 3- minute presentation on my business.
   9. I will achieve my weekly business goal
   10. I will practice today's activity and teach it to my family.
   11. I will add to my savings- even a coin or two.
   12. I will report to my action partner.

_____  _____
My signature               My action partner's signature

(H) HOW WILL I REPORT MY PROGRESS?

1. I have kept separate records.
2. I have paid myself a wage separate from business money.
3. I have prepared my business presentation.
4. I have achieved my weekly business goal.
5. I have practiced the business principles and taught it to my family.
6. I have added to my savings.
7. I have reported to my action partner.
8. I am becoming more self- reliant.

## WEEK 6: HOW IS MY BUSINESS PROGRESSING?

### (A) DID I KEEP MY COMMITMENTS.

1. I will learn from keeping separate records for personal and business money.
2. I will understand how this will help my business.
3. I will learn by paying myself a wage and keep it separate from my business.
4. I will understand how this will help my business.
5. I will learn by working on my weekly business goal.
6. In my business notebook, I will write what I have learnt by keeping my commitments.

### (B) HOW DO I DESCRIBE MY BUSINESS?

1. I will make my business presentation.
2. When I describe my business to others, I learn things about my business that may help me improve.
3. During and after the presentation, I will write my ideas in my business notebook.
4. When I explain my business to others, I seek ideas from them on how to grow my business.
5. Successful business owners improve something every day.

## MY BUSINESS IN THREE MINUTES- INSTRUCTIONS.

PART 1: In less than one minute, describe your business.

PART 2: In less than one minute, describe how answering one of the questions greatly improved your business.

1. What do people want to buy?
2. How do I sell?
3. How do I control costs?
4. How do I increase profits?
5. How do I run my business?

PART 3: In less than 1 minute, describe one thing you will do to continue improving your business. Ask each other questions.

( C) WHAT DO I LEARN?

1. Successful business owners learn continually.
2. I will learn from others, things that will improve my business.
3. I will learn how to grow my business.
4. I will prepare my business income and expense log for last 2 weeks.
5. I will prepare my business income statement for the last 2 weeks.
6. I will help others with their income and expense logs and business income statements. This will be good practice for me.

(D ) AM I BECOMING MORE SELF- RELIANT?

1. My goal is to be self-reliant. Making my business to succeed is only part of that goal.
2. There are changes I have seen in my life as I practice and teach the principles that I have learnt.
3. I am closer to achieving my self- reliant income.
4. I know the things to do to improve.

( E ) WHAT SHOULD I DO TO IMPROVE.

1. I know the ideas that will help my business the most this week.
2. I will make these ideas , my weekly business goal.
3. I will add my weekly business goal to my commitments.
4. I will share my weekly business goal with others.

(F) HOW WILL I MAKE DAILY PROGRESS?

1. I will choose an action partner.

2. I will decide when and how we will contact each other.

3. I will record my action partner's name and contact information.

4. I will read my commitments aloud to my action partner.

5. I promise to keep my commitments by signing my signature below.

MY COMMITMENTS

    5. I will prepare my income and expense log in my business notebook.
    6. I will achieve my weekly business goal.
    7. I will practice today's business principles and teach them to my family.
    8. I will add to my savings – even a coin or two.
    9. I will report to my action partner.

_____           _____

My Signature                                    Action partner's Signature.

(G) HOW WILL I REPORT MY PROGRESS?

1. I have prepared my income and expense logs.

2. I achieved my weekly business goal.

3. I practiced the business principles and taught them to my family.

4. I added to my savings.

5. I will report to my action partner.

WEEK 7: HOW WILL I GROW MY BUSINESS?

(A) DID I KEEP MY COMMITMENTS?

    1. I am working hard to be self-reliant.
    2. I have tried some ideas on my business.
    3. I have learnt some things on trying those ideas.
    4. I have learnt some things working on my weekly business goal.

## (B) WHAT WILL HELP MY BUSINESS MAKE MORE MONEY?

1. An asset is something a business owns that is valuable.
2. I can buy and sell assets. For example; Maria could buy a chair to sit on when selling eggs and she could sell a chicken. These are assets.
3. A productive asset makes money for a business. Maria's hens are productive assets because they produce eggs which maria sells for money. A chair is an asset. It doesn't make money.
4. Successful business owners use productive assets to grow their business.
5. A sewing machine or bicycle can be a productive asset.
6. I can list the productive assets in my business.
7. I can use productive assets to grow my business.
8. I will identify the assets I have and determine how to make them more productive.
9. I will identify and prioritize other assets I need.

## (c) HOW CAN I MAKE MY ASSETS MORE PRODUCTIVE

1. I must use assets wisely.
2. I take care of my assets so that they can be very productive.
3. My business will not progress, if I did not take care of my productive assets e.g. Sewing machine, Broken bicycle, and hen.
4. I need to use my assets as productive as possible.
5. I will be a wise steward with my productive asset. I can make my assets to be more productive.

### GLORIA SEWING SHOP

Gloria had one sewing machine. She took good care of it. She could sew five shirts each day. Her customers wanted more shirts. She taught of hiring a helper and buying another sewing machine.

But instead of buying another sewing machine, Gloria hired a friend to sew with Gloria's machine during the night.

Now, Gloria's business is able to make 10 shirts each day with one sewing machine.

1. How was Gloria a wise steward with her productive asset?
2. How can you make your asset more profitable.

( D ) HOW CAN I GET MORE PRODUCTIVE ASSETS?

1. I will think of assets that I could get that would help me grow my business and list them below. I will discuss why these assets would help my business grow.

| TYPE OF ASSETS | ASSETS I HAVE | NEW ASSETS THAT COULD HELP GROW MY BUSINESS |
|---|---|---|
| Tools / Machine | | |
| Vehicle | | |
| Building | | |
| Animal | | |
| Other | | |

How could you get the assets you listed above. Below is a list of ways business people get new assets. Discuss their advantages and disadvantages.

WAYS TO GET NEW ASSETS: ADVANTAGES: DISADVANTAGES.

1. Save to buy an asset.
2. Get a partner who has an asset.
3. Rent an asset.
4. Borrow an asset.
5. Get a loan to buy an asset.
6. Other.
7. I know the asset that would be the most useful to my business right now.
8. I know how much money it will help me to make.
9. I know how easy it will be to get.

10. I know some of the ways I could pay for the new asset.

( E ) HOW CAN I CONTROL COSTS?

1. Productive assets help our businesses make money. To grow our businesses, we also need to control costs. But not all expenses are the same.
2. Variable costs increase or decrease with sales.
3. Fixed costs must be paid no matter how much or how little we sell.
4. Successful business owners only add fixed costs when they know they will help the business make more money.

DANIEL'S BUSINESS EXPENSES

(Circle fixed or Variable for each expense)

Rent for shop   = Fixed variable.

Wood for furniture = Fixed variable.

Delivery costs= Fixed  variable.

Daniel's wage = Fixed variable.

5. List your own business expenses .
6. Circle variable and fixed for each expense.
7. Record your income and expenses.
8. Show which are fixed and which are variable.
9. Prepare your income statement.

( F ) WHAT SHOULD I DO TO IMPROVE?

1. I will ponder what I am learning.
2. I will write my impressions in my business notebook.
3. I will find the idea that will help my business the most this week.
4. I will make the idea my weekly business goal.
5. I will add my weekly business goal to my commitment.
6. I will share my weekly business goal and impressions with others.

( G ) HOW WILL I MAKE PROGRESS?

1. I will choose my action partner.

2. I will decide when and how we will contact each other.
3. I will record my action partner's name and contact information.
4. I will read each commitment aloud to my action partner.
5. I promise to keep my commitments by signing my signature below.

MY COMMITMENTS
6. I will write a plan to make my current assets more productive.
7. I will identify the most important new productive assets I need for my business.
8. I will prepare my income statements with fixed and variable expenses.
9. I will achieve my weekly business goal.
10. I will practice today's business principles and teach it to my family.
11. I will add to my savings – even a coin or two.
12. I will report to my action partner.

_____        _____
My Signature                  Action partner's signature.

( H ) HOW WILL I REPORT MY PROGRESS?

1. I will write a plan to make my assets to be more productive.
2. I will identify most important new assets.
3. I will prepare my income statements.
4. I will achieve my weekly business goal.
5. I will practice the business principles and teach them to my family.
6. I will add to my savings.
7. I will report to my action partner.

FIXED COSTS AND VARIABLE COSTS.

(8) I should be careful of fixed costs because they remain the same whether we sell or not e.g: rent.

(9) We should choose the productive asset that is of the highest priority to our business right now.

# WEEK 8: HOW MUCH CAN I AFFORD TO INVEST TO GROW MY BUSINESS?

## ( A ) DID I KEEP MY COMMITMENTS?

1. I will report on my commitments.
2. I know how to make my assets to be more productive.
3. I know how to maintain my assets.
4. I know the productive asset that is my highest priority.
5. I know why it is my highest priority.
6. I know my fixed and variable expenses.
7. It helps to know the difference between fixed and variable costs.
8. I should be careful of fixed costs because it remains the same whether we sell or not.
9. I will record what I have learnt by working on my weekly business goal.
10. I will record what I have learnt by keeping my commitments in my business notebook.

## ( B ) CAN I AFFORD MORE ASSETS?

1. One way to grow our businesses is to add productive assets.
2. Before we add productive assets to our businesses, we need to know if we can afford it.
3. Successful business owners make sure that they can afford improvements to their businesses before they make them.
4. Successful business owners make investments wisely.
5. I will find out if I can afford a loan to buy an asset.
6. I will create cash flow statements to better understand the future of my business.
7. A cash flow statement is a tool that helps you look at your business so that you can identify ways to grow your business.
8. There are three steps for creating a cash flow statement.

STEP 1: Using your past income statements, look at your business past performances.

STEP 2: Look at the future of your business by asking yourself this question, "What will my income and expenses be in the future".

STEP 3: Figure out the available cash you will have in the future.

A cash flow statement can help you decide between different ways to grow your business, such as adding to your product selection, decreasing your expenses, increasing your income and evaluating possible loans.

( C ) HOW MUCH CASH IS AVAILABLE CURRENTLY?

1. To know if I have enough cash to grow my business, I need to know these things: the past, the future, and the cash flow.
2. I can find out these three things by creating a cash flow statement.

STEP 1: THE PAST

Using my income statements, I will write down my income, fixed expenses, variable expenses , and profit and loss for the last two months.

| INCOME | 2 months ago | Last month | This month | Next month | Month 3 | Month 4 | Month 5 | Month 6 |
|---|---|---|---|---|---|---|---|---|
| Fixed expenses | 4400 | 4400 | | | | | | |
| Profit ( or loss) | -3300 | -3300 | | | | | | |
| Starting cash | -1000 | -1000 | | | | | | |
| Available cash | 100 | 100 | | | | | | |
| | | | | | | | | |
| | | | | | | | | |

What does the cash flow statement for the last two months say about my (Maria's) business?

STEP 2: THE FUTURE

51

On the next month column below, based on the numbers from the past two months, Maria writes what she thinks her future income, fixed expenses, variable expenses, and profit and loss will be.

Maria doesn't plan to make any change to her business, so she thinks her income and expenses for the next six months will be the same as the last two months.

Look at Maria's cash flow statement below. Do Maria's monthly profits change.

| INCOME | 4400 | 4400 | 4400 | 4400 | 4400 | 4400 | 4400 | 4400 | 4400 |
|---|---|---|---|---|---|---|---|---|---|
| Fixed expenses | 3300 | 3300 | 3300 | 3300 | 3300 | 3300 | 3300 | 3300 | 3300 |
| Variable expenses | 1000 | 1000 | 1000 | 1000 | 1000 | 1000 | 1000 | 1000 | 1000 |
| Profit (or loss) | 100 | 100 | 100 | 100 | 100 | 100 | 100 | 100 | 100 |
| Starting cash | | | | | | | | | |
| Available cash | | | | | | | | | |

### STEP 3: AVAILABLE CASH

Starting cash (50) is what Maria has in the bank at the start of the month. In this case he starts with 50. Each month, she adds her monthly profits to her starting cash to get her available cash (50 +100 = 150). The available cash becomes the starting cash for the next month (150).

Look at the cash flow statement below, how much does Maria have available at the end of the six months?

Now that Maria knows how much cash she might have available over the next six months, she can decide between the different ways to grow her business.

| | 2 MONTHS AGO | LAST MONTH | THIS MONTH | NEXT MONTH | MONTH 3 | MONTH 4 | MONTH 5 | MONTH 6 |
|---|---|---|---|---|---|---|---|---|
| INCOME | 4400 | 4400 | 4400 | 4400 | 4400 | 4400 | 4400 | 4400 |

| Fixed expenses | -3300 | -3300 | -3300 | -3300 | -3300 | -3300 | -3300 | -3300 |
|---|---|---|---|---|---|---|---|---|
| Variable expenses | -1000 | -1000 | -1000 | -1000 | -1000 | -1000 | -1000 | -1000 |
| Profit (or loss) | 100 | 100 | 100 | 100 | 100 | 100 | 100 | 100 |
| Starting cash | 50 | 150 | 250 | 350 | 450 | 550 | 650 | 750 |
| Profit (or loss) | 100 | 100 | 100 | 100 | 100 | 100 | 100 | 100 |
| Available cash | 150 | 250 | 350 | 450 | 550 | 650 | 750 | 850 |

( D ) HOW MUCH CASH IS AVAILABLE FOR LOAN PAYMENTS?

Now let's see what happens to Maria's cash flow, if she borrows 1500 for 6 months to buy 15 chickens. Look at Maria's cash flow statement below. Does Maria have enough cash flow for loan payments of 275?. What is Maria's available cash? What should Maria do? Should Maria try a different loan amount? Could she save and pay cash for the chickens?

MARIA'S CASH FLOW STATEMENT

1. INCOME/ THIS MONTH: Because she will have more eggs, Maria thinks that each month she will have about 900 more in income (60 more in income per chicken times 15), 900 plus her current income of 4400 is 5300
2. FIXED EXPENSES /NEXT MONTH: She thinks her fixed expenses would increase to 3500 ( 20 more to rent a bike plus her existing expense of 3300).
3. LOAN AMOUNT/MONTH 5: If she takes the loan, she will also have a fixed expense of 275 . (350 the first month).

4. **VARIABLE EXPENSES / THIS MONTH:** She thinks that her variable expenses will increase to 1600 because of 500 more in chicken feed and 100 for her niece to deliver the eggs.
5. **AVAILABLE CASH/ NEXT MONTH:** In the first two months, Maria has enough available cash to make the loan payment.
6. **AVAILABLE CASH/ MONTH 4:** However, look at the last four months of the loan (months 3-6). Will Maria have enough money to make all of her loan payments?
7. **PROFIT (OR LOSS)/ MONTH 8:** After Maria has paid off the loan, her profits go back up. But, is it too late?

|  | 2 MONTHS AGO | LAST MONTH | THIS MONTH | NEXT MONTH | MONTH 3 | MONTH 4 | MONTH 5 | MONTH 6 | MONTH 7 |
|---|---|---|---|---|---|---|---|---|---|
| INCOME | 4400 | 4400 | 5300 | 5300 | 5300 | 5300 | 5300 | 5300 | 5300 |
| Fixed expenses | -3300 | -3300 | - | - | - | - | -3500 | - | - |
|  |  |  | 3500 | 3500 | 3500 | 3500 |  | 3500 | 3500 |
| Loan payment |  |  | -350 | -275 | -275 | -275 | -275 | -275 |  |
| Variable expenses | -1000 | -1000 | - | - | - | - | -1600 | - | - |
|  |  |  | 1600 | 1600 | 1600 | 1600 |  | 1600 | 1600 |
| Profit (or loss) | 100 | 100 | -150 | -75 | -75 | -75 | -75 | -75 | 200 |
| Starting cash | 50 | 150 | 250 | 100 | 25 | -50 | -125 | -200 | -275 |
| Profit (or loss) | 100 | 100 | -150 | -75 | -75 | -75 | -75 | -75 | 200 |
| Available cash | 100 | 250 | 100 | 25 | -50 | -125 | -200 | -275 | -75 |

Can she afford more assets?

1. Now let's see what happens if Maria gets a loan for a smaller amount: 800 for 6 months to buy 8 chickens. Look at Maria's cash flow statement to the right. Does Maria have enough cash flow for a loan of 800?. What is Maria's

available cash? Could Maria handle a larger loan amount? Should she get a larger loan?
2. In this example, Maria is using her cash flow statement to decide if she can afford new chickens. She could also use the cash flow statement to decide on different changes to her business such as renting a bike, buying a new sign, or buying different feed.

MARIA'S CASH- FLOW STATEMENT

1. INCOME /THIS MONTH: Maria thinks that with 8 new chickens, she will have about 480 more in income (60 more in income per chicken times 8). 480 plus her current income of 4400 is 4880.
2. FIXED EXPENSES/ NEXT MONTH: She thinks that her fixed expenses will not increase because she will not rent a bike.
3. LOAN PAYMENT/ MONTH 5: If she takes this loan, Maria will have a fixed expense of 150 (250 the first month).
4. VARIABLE EXPENSES/ THIS MONTH: She thinks that her variable expenses will increase to 1300 because of 250 more in chicken feed and 50 for her niece to deliver the eggs.
5. AVAILABLE CASH/MONTH 4: Look at her available cash. Will Maria have enough money to make all her loan payments?
6. PROFIT (OR LOSS)/MONTH 7: Look at Maria's profits and losses. Notice that her profits are lower during the loan but are higher than before she got the loan.

|  | 2 MONTHS AGO | LAST MONTH | THIS MONTH | NEXT MONTH | MONTH 3 | MONTH 4 | MONTH 5 | MONTH 6 | MONTH 7 | MONTH 8 |
|---|---|---|---|---|---|---|---|---|---|---|
| INCOME | 4400 | 4400 | 4880 | 4880 | 4880 | 4880 | 4880 | 4880 | 4880 | 4880 |
| Fixed expenses | -3300 | -3300 | -3300 | -3300 | -3300 | -3300 | -3300 | -3300 | -3300 | -3300 |
| Loan payment |  |  | -250 | -150 | -150 | -150 | -150 | -150 |  |  |

| Variable expenses. | -1000 | - 1000 | - 1300 | - 1300 | - 1300 | - 1300 | - 1300 | - 1300 | - 1300 | - 1300 |
|---|---|---|---|---|---|---|---|---|---|---|
| Profit (or loss) | 100 | 100 | 30 | 130 | 130 | 130 | 130 | 130 | 280 | 280 |
| Starting cash | 50 | 150 | 250 | 280 | 410 | 540 | 670 | 800 | 930 | 1210 |
| Profit (or loss) | 100 | 100 | 30 | 130 | 130 | 130 | 130 | 130 | 260 | 280 |
| Available cash | 150 | 250 | 280 | 410 | 540 | 670 | 800 | 930 | 1210 | 1490 |

( E ) HOW MUCH CASH IS AVAILABLE FOR MY BUSINESS?

1. Now make a cash flow statement for your own business in your business notebook.
2. Think of a productive asset you could get for your business.
3. Think about how much more income and expenses you would have.
4. If you don't know what numbers to use or you don't have a business, help someone who does. This is just practice.
5. Talk with lenders and find out what your loan payments will be.
6. Include loan payments in your cash flow statement.
7. How does knowing your available cash help you to make decisions about your business?
8. Besides loan payments, are there other ways that knowing your cash flow can help you grow your business?

MARIA'S CASH FLOW STATEMENT

1. INCOME/ TWO MONTHS AGO: Using your income statements, write your income and expenses from the last two months.

2. INCOME / THIS MONTH: Write what you think your new income will be for the next six months ( previous income plus income from new asset).
3. FIXED EXPENSES/ MONTH 3: Write what you think your new expenses will be for the next six months (previous expenses plus expenses for new asset).
4. LOAN PAYMENT / MONTH 6: You will write your loan payments here, but if you don't know them, yet, leave this line blank for now.
5. PROFIT ( OR LOSS)/ THIS MONTH: Calculate your profits and losses by subtracting your expenses from your income.
6. AVAILABLE CASH/ THIS MONTH: To find out how much available cash you have , your profit to ( or subtract your loss from) the starting cash.
7. AVAILABLE CASH/ MONTH 6: When you find out your loan payment amounts, you can use this cash flow to see if you have enough available cash to make all your loan payments.

|  | Two months ago | Last month | This month | Next month | Month 3 | Month 4 | Month 5 | Month 6 |
|---|---|---|---|---|---|---|---|---|
| INCOME |  |  |  |  |  |  |  |  |
| Fixed expense |  |  |  |  |  |  |  |  |
| Loan payment |  |  |  |  |  |  |  |  |
| Variable expense |  |  |  |  |  |  |  |  |
| Profit (or loss) |  |  |  |  |  |  |  |  |
| Starting cash |  |  |  |  |  |  |  |  |
| Available cash |  |  |  |  |  |  |  |  |
|  |  |  |  |  |  |  |  |  |

( F ) SIX- MONTH CASH FLOW STATEMENTS

1. Create a cash flow statement to show your current business situation.
2. Create a cash flow statement that includes a way to get a new asset.

( G ) WHAT SHOULD I DO TO IMPROVE?

1. I will ponder what I am learning.
2. I will write any impression I have in my business notebook.
3. I will find the idea that will help my business the most this week.
4. I will make that Idea my weekly business goal.
5. I will add my weekly business goal to my commitments.
6. I will share my weekly business goal and other impressions with others.

( H ) HOW WILL I MAKE DAILY PROGRESS?

1. I will choose my action partner.
2. We will decide when and how we will contact each other.
3. I will record my action partner's name and contact information.
4. I will read each commitment aloud to my action partner.
5. I will promise to keep my commitments by signing my signature below.

MY COMMITMENTS.
1. I will create a cash flow statement for my current business situation.
2. I will create a cash flow statement that includes a way to get a new asset.
3. I will achieve my weekly business goal .
4. I will practice today's business principles and teach it to my family.
5. I will add to my savings – even a coin or two.
6. I will report to my action partner.

_____          _____
My Signature                                          Action partner's signature.

( I ) HOW WILL I REPORT MY PROGRESS?

1. I created a cash flow for my current business situation.
2. I created a cash flow for a way to get a new asset.
3. I achieved my weekly business goal.

4. I practiced the business principles I learnt and taught them to my family.
5. I added to my savings.
6. I reported to my action partner.
7. I will make a list of lenders in my area.
8. I will know the monthly loan payments.
9. I will make sure that I have enough available cash each month to make the payments.
10. I will know by creating cash flow statements to better understand the future of my business.
11. I can try with a smaller loan if I can afford it.

WEEK 9: HOW DO I KNOW IF I SHOULD USE A LOAN TO GROW MY BUSINESS?

( A ) DID I KEEP MY COMMITMENTS?

1. I will know what my cash flow tell me about my business.
2. I will find out if I have enough cash available to make loan payments or do other things to improve my business.
3. I learnt a lot by working on my weekly business goal.
4. I will record what I have learnt by keeping my commitments in my business notebook.

( B ) IS BORROWING MONEY GOOD OR BAD?

1. I will think of someone I know who borrowed money.
2. I will find out if borrowing money helped them or hurt them.
3. Personal household debt and business debt is different.
4. Personal loans are used to spend more than we have means to pay.
5. Business loans are used to produce more than we have means to produce.
6. Some debt- such as for a modest home, expenses for education, may be necessary. But never should we enter into financial bondage through consumer debt without carefully weighing the costs.
7. Now, I do not mean to say that all debt is bad, of course not. Sound business debt is one of the elements of growth.
8. How do I know if I should use a loan to grow my business?

9. I will talk with at least 10 customers to learn if they would buy more if I had more to sell.
10. I will visit at least four lenders and ask them the questions on the loan terms worksheet.
11. I will learn and practice skills to help me know if borrowing money is a good idea for my business.

( C ) HOW WILL THE "FOUR RIGHTS" HELP ME DECIDE?

1. I will get a loan.
2. I will find out if a loan would help me or crush me.
3. I will read aloud and discuss each of the "four rights".

THE FOUR RIGHTS

1. RIGHT REASON: Borrow only if it will help my business make more money.
2. RIGHT TIME: Borrow only if I have been in business long enough to know my business well and can show that enough people will buy what I am selling.
3. RIGHT TERMS: Borrow only if I can find a good lender.
4. RIGHT AMOUNT: Borrow only if I can show that I know that I can pay back.

ANSWER "YES" OR "NO" OR NOT SURE.

(A ) REASONS FOR BORROWING

1. Am I borrowing for productive business (not personal ) reasons?
2. Will the things I buy with the loan make me money immediately?
3. Is getting a loan better than saving cash to grow my business?
4. Have I thought about all the risks?

( B ) TIME FOR BORROWING

1. Have I been in business long enough to know my business well?
2. Is this part of a plan I have to grow my business?
3. Can I show that customers will buy more if I have more to sell ?

4. If I buy something for my business ( like a chicken or truck ) will it last longer than the loan?

( C ) TERMS FOR BORROWING

1. Can I list three to five good lenders?
2. Do I know the true cost of the loan?
3. Can I explain all the terms of the loan?
4. Can I explain why one lender is better than another?

( D ) AMOUNT FOR BORROWING

1. Have I made a six-month cash flow statement?
2. Can I make a payment and still make money?
3. If I don't have extra sales, can I still make the payment?

( a ) I have learnt how to use cash flow statement to know if I will have enough available cash to make payments. This will help me to know if I am borrowing the right amount.

( b ) After meeting the lenders, I will use the cash flow worksheet to make sure I can afford the payment.

( c ) I do not need help creating a cash flow statement.

( d ) If I am not sure about the answer to one of the four rights questions,

( e ) I will make a plan to find the answer .

( f ) Before I borrow, I should also find out the answers if I am not sure.

( g ) I will ask others for help if needed.

( D ) SHOULD I BORROW FOR MY BUSINESS?

The tools to use during the week to gather information and make decisions are the four rights checklist, loan terms worksheet, lender information and the six- month cash flow.

( 1 ) FOUR RIGHTS CHECKLIST

During the week, review these questions and check them off when you can answer yes.

( 2 ) LOAN TERMS WORKSHEET

During the week, use the loan terms worksheet to learn about at least three lenders.

( 3 ) LENDER INFORMATION

This contains a list of possible lenders. Ask other business owners for suggestions of good lenders in your area. During the week, use this information to find and contact lenders.

( 4 ) SIX – MONTH CASH FLOW

Use this worksheet to create cash flow statements to know which loans you can afford.

( E ) WHAT SHOULD I DO TO IMPROVE?

1. I will quietly ponder on what I am learning.
2. I will record any impression I have in my business notebook.
3. I will find which idea that will help my business the most this week.
4. I will add this idea to my business goal.
5. I will add my business goal to my commitments.
6. I will share my weekly goal and other impressions with others.

( F ) HOW WILL I MAKE DAILY PROGRESS?

1. I will choose an action partner.
2. I will decide when and how we will contact each other.
3. I will record my action partner's name and contact information.
4. I will read each commitment aloud to my action partner.
5. I will promise to keep my commitments by signing my signature below.

   MY COMMITMENTS
1. I will talk to at least four lenders using the loan terms worksheet.

2. I will use the questions on the four rights checklist to see if getting a loan now is right for me.
3. I will use my cash flow statements to evaluate my loan options.
4. I will achieve my weekly business goal.
5. I will practice today's business principles and teach it to my family.
6. I will add to my savings- even a coin or two.
7. I will report to my action partner.

    _____         _____
    My Signature                       Action partner's signature.

( G ) HOW WILL I REPORT MY PROGRESS?

1. During the week, I will record my progress.
2. I will record the number of times I kept my commitment.
3. I talked to at least four lenders.
4. I used cash flow statements to evaluate loan options.
5. I used the four rights checklist.
6. I achieved my weekly business goal.
7. I practiced the business principles I learnt and taught them to my family.
8. I added to my savings.
9. I reported to my action partner.
10. I will only get a loan if I have the four rights.

RIGHT REASON:

1. My reason for borrowing has to be for business and not for personal reasons.
2. A loan should be for things you can sell right away or something that produces immediately.
3. Remember you have to start repaying loans immediately.
4. With cash, you save now and buy later- less growth but less risk. With a loan , you buy now and pay later- more growth and more risk.
5. I know how I can reduce the risk therefore I think I have the right reason to take a loan.

RIGHT TIME.

1. I have been long in this business and it has been going on well.
2. Some people get loans for businesses they have just barely started – that is very risky.
3. I am confident that customers will buy more if I have more to sell.
4. I am going to talk to customers and make a list of everyone who would buy. I am going to talk to at least 10 of them.
5. If I decide to get a loan, a list of future customers will help me show the lender , I understand exactly how I will use the loan.
6. My business will produce till the next two years and I plan to get a six-month loan.

RIGHT TERMS

1. I will compare the terms of many lenders before I take a loan.
2. I will use the lender's worksheet to help me ask good questions.
3. I will learn about possible penalties, interest rates, fees and commissions, upfront fees and weekend payments.
4. I will compare the lenders that had flat interest rates and declining interest rates and find the difference.
5. If the rates are the same, declining is better than flat to help me find the right terms.

RIGHT AMOUNT

1. I must have enough cash flow before I take a loan.
2. Cash flow is money moving in and out of your business.
3. I must have enough money coming in to cover the loan payments.
4. I know that if I did not sell as much as I expected, I will be late in some payments.
5. I know that if I am late in some payments, the penalties will add up and make it harder for me to make payments.
6. That is why I need a six-month cash flow statement before deciding on a loan.
7. I have created a six-month cash flow of my business .

8. A cash flow statement helps to know if I can afford to make the loan payments each month.
9. I have income statements for the last two months.
10. When you create a cash flow statement, you will know if you are borrowing the right amount.

FOUR RIGHTS CHECKLIST

ANSWER YES , NO OR NOT SURE

RIGHT REASON

1. Am I borrowing for a productive business (not personal ) reason.
2. Is a loan better than cash to grow my business?
3. Will the things I buy with the loan make me money immediately.
4. Do I know everything that could go wrong?

RIGHT TIME

1. Have I been in business long enough to know the business well.
2. Is this part of a plan I have to grow my business?
3. Can I prove customers will buy more if have more to sell?
4. If I buy something for my business (like a chicken or a truck), will it last longer than my loan?

RIGHT TERMS.

1. Can I list three to five good lenders?
2. Do I know the true cost of the loan?
3. Can I explain all of the terms of the loan?
4. Can I explain why one lender is better than another.

RIGHT AMOUNT

1. Have I made a six-month cash flow statement?
2. Can I make a payment and still make money?

LOAN TERMS WORKSHEET

I will take this loan terms worksheet with me when I visit lenders. I will ask the lenders questions 1- 4.

I will ask myself questions 5-6.

1. QUALIFICATIONS: What do I need to give or show you (the lenders) to get a loan?
2. PAYMENT FREQUENCY: When is the first payment due? How often do I need to make payments? Can I have a copy of the repayment schedule?
3. PENALTIES: Are there fees or penalties if I do not pay on time.
4. DIRECT COSTS: If I borrow 100, 1000 or 10,000 (pick one amount based on local currency and use it for each lender), how much do I pay after I have paid off the loan, including all interest, fees , etc. If I borrow enough for one asset, for example; one chicken, how much extra do I pay by getting the loan? How much are the upfront fees? How much is each payment? Is this a flat or declining interest rate?
5. INDIRECT COSTS: How much time does it take to make payments? How much does it cost me to go to the lender to pay?
6. TRUE COST OF THE LOAN: What is the total of the direct costs and indirect costs of the loan? ( Add the costs from questions 4 and 5).

SIX- MONTH CASH FLOW STATEMENT

1. I will copy this cash flow worksheet into my business notebook.
2. I will use one for each lender to see if I can afford the loan terms. I will learn about it this week.

Lender's Name: _____

|  | TWO MONTHS AGO | LAST MONTH | THIS MONTH | NEXT MONTH | MONTH 3 | MONTH 4 | MONTH 5 | MONTH 6 |
|---|---|---|---|---|---|---|---|---|
| Total income |  |  |  |  |  |  |  |  |
| Fixed expense |  |  |  |  |  |  |  |  |
| Loan |  |  |  |  |  |  |  |  |

|  |  |  |  |  |  |  |  |  |
|---|---|---|---|---|---|---|---|---|
| payments |  |  |  |  |  |  |  |  |
| Variable payments |  |  |  |  |  |  |  |  |
| Total profit/loss |  |  |  |  |  |  |  |  |
| Starting cash |  |  |  |  |  |  |  |  |
| Available cash |  |  |  |  |  |  |  |  |

WEEK 10: HOW WILL I ATTRACT MORE CUSTOMERS AND CLOSE SALES?

( A ) DID I KEEP MY COMMITMENTS?

1. I will write what I have learnt by keeping my commitments in my business notebook.
2. I will record what I have learnt by talking to lenders.
3. I will find out if a loan is right for me now.
4. I will find out if I have the right reason, right time , right terms and right amount for me to take a loan.
5. I will record what I have learnt by keeping my weekly business goal in my business notebook.

( B ) WHY WOULD CUSTOMERS WANT TO BUY FROM ME?

1. To grow our businesses, we need to attract more customers and sell more. People spend their money for something they value. The more they value something, the more they will pay for it.
2. To sell successfully, we need to know what our customers value, attract those customers and sell them the value.
3. We need to offer more value than our competition.
4. I will learn about the things customers value.
5. I will learn about how to attract customers and close sales.
6. I will test my marketing ideas and track results.
7. I will learn from customers and test solutions to customer's problems.
8. I am able to describe my customers.
9. I can do that in a specific way.
10. I know their age and gender.
11. I know their income.
12. I know when and where they buy my product.
13. I know why they buy my product;
    (a) I make it convenient for them to buy
    (b) I am friendly.
    (c) I call my customers by their names.
14. I know the value I will provide that competitors do not offer.
15. I have a better price.
16. I have a better location.
17. I have a better selection.
18. These are called my competitive advantage.
19. These are what makes my customers choose my business over the competition.
20. Successful business owners know why customers buy their products.
21. Successful business owners understand their customers by asking good questions to learn more about their problems and how they can help.

( C ) ASKING GOOD QUESTIONS

1. I will find out the things I want to know about my customers.
2. I will find out the problems my customers came to me to solve.
3. I will find out the questions I could ask to find out . Example:

It looks like you are in a middle of a project and have a problem. How can I help?
4. I will share my questions with others.
5. I will find out the things my customer is ready to buy.
6. I will know what I could ask to find out.
7. I will find out if it is for a special occasion.
8. I will find out when the special occasion will take place.
9. I will share with others, the things I need to know about my customers.
10. I will share the questions I would ask to find out.
11. I will discuss ways to learn more about my customers and what I can do this week to start learning.

( D ) HOW WILL I ATTRACT MORE CUSTOMERS?

1. I will think about times when I bought something at a business I had never been to before.
2. I will find out what attracted me to those businesses.
3. I will find out how businesses attract customers in my area.

( E ) WHAT ATTRACTED ME? WHY DID I BUY? PRODUCT OR SERVICE I BOUGHT.

1. CANDY- Personal selling: Business owner told me about it.
   Referral: A neighbor said that I should try it.
   Sale: 20% off the price/ Buy one and get one for half price.
2. CLOTHING: Personal selling: Sales person told me about it.
   Ad: I saw a poster on a wall. Sale: Buy one and get one for half price.
3. VEGETABLES: Referral: Friend told me to try it.
   Ad: I saw it in the newspaper.   Order Sample.
4. I will share with others what I have written.
5. I will find the methods that could work for my business.
6. Businesses do not attract customers by accident . They came up with ideas on how to market their product or service.
7. They got the ideas on marketing about how to find and influence customers.
8. They got ideas on marketing about what we hope customers will do. Eg; MARKETING IDEAS: IDEA: If I give out samples.

9. EXPECTED RESULT: People will buy more candy.
10. I will think of ideas to help more customers find my business and buy what I sell.
11. I will discuss the most effective methods in my area.
12. I will write out the results I expect. EXAMPLE:

MARKETING IDEAS: IDEA; If I use loud speaker to tell people that my chairs are 40% off. EXPECTED RESULT: Customers will come to my shop and buy chairs.

( F ) HOW WILL I TEST MY MARKETING PLAN?

1. I will find out if my ideas worked.
2. I need a way to test my ideas to test if they worked.
3. I need a way to measure results.
4. I will discuss and write several marketing ideas and results I want for my business .
5. I will include any areas that seem to be working now.
6. For each idea, I will write how I would measure results.
7. I know that my ideas will change and improve over time as I try them out and measure them.

( G ) TESTING MY MARKETING IDEAS.

IDEA: If I use a loudspeaker to tell people my chairs are 40% off.

EXPECTED RESULT: Customers will come to my shop and buy chairs.

MEASUREMENT: When customers come in , I will ask how they heared about the 40% off sale. I will keep a log of customer responses.

1. I will go and test my ideas this week.
2. I do not need to test all my ideas at the same time.
3. It is possible that some ideas won't work. That is okay.
4. I will just keep trying ideas and measuring results.
5. I will find the best ways to help people discover us and buy what we sell.

( H ) HOW WILL I GET CUSTOMERS TO BUY?

1. I will find out why some some customers buy and others choose not to buy.
2. I know that there are many reasons but I can influence that decision.
3. I will find out why some business owners are unable to convince the customers to buy something.
4. I will think of myself and my customers.
5. To convince customers to buy, we must ask , listen and suggest.
   I MUST ASK
   1. What does the customer really want.
   2. Why does the customer want it.
      I MUST LISTEN
      Do I really listen?

I MUST SUGGEST

Do I have options that will benefit both me and the customer? Successful business owners use this cycle to convince more customers to buy their products and services.

1. I will do things differently this time to get a better result.
2. I will think about times when someone convinced me to make a decision even when you were'nt planning to.
3. I will find out what the person said that made me to buy.
4. Approaches that we can use to convince our customers to buy our products is called closing the sale.
5. I will practice closing the sale with people by selling my product to them.
6. I will list the best close I can use to sell to my customers.
7. I will write suggestions for each type of closing of sale.

( I) CLOSING THE SALE

( a ) TWO GOOD OPTIONS: Would you like bananas or mangoes?

(b) IF: If I can get that price would you like me to order it.

(c ) IMPORTANT EVENT: I can have this ready before your wife's birthday.

( d ) SAMPLE: Try this, I think you will like the flavor of this one better.

( e ) OTHER: What if you were to get both pairs of shoes and I gave you discount.

( 8 ) I will try out the different approaches .

( 9 ) I will discuss what I think will be the best approach for getting my customers to make a purchase from my business.

( 10 ) I will find out why it is the best approach for my customers.

( 11 ) Successful business owners close the sale.

( J ) HOW WILL I MAKE IT EASY TO KEEP BUYING?

( 1 ) Successful business owners make it easy and enjoyable for customers to buy from them.

( 2 ) I will make my customers to like the prices, selection and me.

3. I will make customers to find it easy to find what they want.
4. I will answer their question.
5. I will make them to like the place.
6. I will be helpful to my customers. Customers keep coming back to businesses when the owner and workers know their customer's name , smile at their customers, listen and respond to customer's needs.
7. I will find out the things I need to do in my business to better keep my customers coming back.
8. I will find out the things I will add to the list above.

( K ) WHAT SHOULD I DO TO IMPROVE?

1. I will write down my impressions in my business notebook.
2. I will find the idea that will help my business the most this week.
3. I will make the idea my weekly business goal.
4. I will add my weekly business goal to my commitments.
5. I will share my impressions and weekly business goal with others.

( L ) HOW WILL I MAKE DAILY PROGRESS?

1. I will choose my action partner.

2. We will decide when and how we can contact each other.
3. I will record my action partners name and contact information.
4. I will read each commitment aloud to my action partner.
5. I will promise to keep my commitment by signing my commitment below.
   MY COMMITMENTS.
   1. I will talk to at least five customers to learn what they want from my business.
   2. I will test at least two marketing ideas and track results.
   3. I will practice closing the sale with at least 10 customers and learn which approach works best.
   4. I will achieve my weekly business goal.
   5. I will practice today's business principle and teach it to my family.
   6. I will add to my savings- even a coin or two.
   7. I will report to my action partner.

_____          _____

My Signature                    Action partner's signature.

( M ) HOW WILL I REPORT MY PROGRESS?

1. I will record the number of times I kept my commitment.
2. I talked to at least five customers.
3. I tested at least two marketing ideas and track results.
4. I will practice closing the sale at least 10 times.
5. I achieved my weekly business goal.
6. I practiced business principles and taught it to my family.
7. I added to my savings.
8. I reported to my action partner.

It will be a great match if you find a successful business and you are a great salesman. Remember your market research with customers- what they liked, the time of day, the locations, how they purchased with friends- what mattered to them. What mattered to them is solving their problems.

- Choose the right time.

- Choose the right location( where many people spend time together).
- Play some happy music to draw attention and even sang with it in a definite unique way to make people at least start to smile.
- Pass a few free samples to women who are surrounded with friends and then asked them how they liked it. That worked.
- As sales picks up, increase price and no one will complain.
- Try discounts if it will not cut off profits or decrease sales.
- Find out what customers did not like.
- Think of new marketing ideas and how to increase sales.
- Think of how to add value for your customers.
- Make customers to find it convenient to buy from you.
- Making your customers happy must be important to you.
- I have learnt a lot talking to my customers and other business owners.
- Friends can help with some marketing ideas.
- In marketing, start by thinking more about your customers and how to find more people like them . Test some ideas and find three that really work. Keep trying and testing.
- You can work on some marketing ideas without buying anything like business cards.
- Ask, listen and suggest for you to sell. ( ASK, LISTEN, SUGGEST).

WEEK 11: HOW WILL I INCREASE MY PROFITS?

(A ) DID I KEEP MY COMMITMENTS?

1. I will report on my commitments.
2. I will record what I learnt talking to my customers in my business notebook.
3. I will record what I learnt as I tested my marketing ideas.
4. I will record what I have learnt as I practice closing the sale.
5. I will learn by working on my weekly business goal.
6. I will write what I have learnt by keeping my commitments in my business notebook.

( B ) HOW WILL I SELL MORE?

1. I will make the sale.
2. I will not miss the sale.

3. Adding a delivery service will make me to sell more or " up sell".

" Upselling " means giving out customers the option of buying more or better products than they were going to buy.

MORE: Offer a drink or bread to a customer who ordered dry fish.

BETTER: Offer a higher quality sewing machine to a customer who is thinking of buying a lower quality sewing machine.

4. I will find out how to upsell.
5. II will list examples of upselling that I have seen.
6. I will find out how I can increase profits.
7. I will try two ways to upsell.
8. I will try two ways to lower my costs.

( C ) WHAT SHOULD I UPSELL?

Customers won't buy something more just because we suggest it. It must be something they want more than the original product. They may be willing to pay more for such things as saving time, relationships, saving money, speed, quality, reliability , quantity, beauty, service and reputation.

1. I will find out what my customers pay more for.
2. I will determine the ways I will use to find out.
3. I will get a partner and discuss what I think my customers value.
4. I will list three ways I can use to find out what my customers value eg; MY IDEA ABOUT WHAT MY CUSTOMERS VALUE.

I think my customers value reliability.

WHAT I WILL ASK OR DO TO FIND OUT.

I will ask customers: if I guarantee delivery by 5:00 every time, would you be interested.

MY IDEA ABOUT WHAT MY CUSTOMERS VALUE.

I think my customers might value reliability.

WHAT I WILL ASK OR DO TO FIND OUT.

I will label one box of fruit " Picked fresh this morning" and another box " Picked this week" . Watch which customers choose.

After writing my ideas, I will share them with others. Successful business owners know what their customers value.

( D ) WHAT SHOULD MY UPSELL PRICE BE?

1. I know that a customer may want something more.
2. I will know the price he or she is willing to pay.
3. I will know what price I am willing to sell.
4. I know that I have to make a profit.
5. I have tested my idea that my customers valued quality.
6. My customers usually chose the fruit that was "picked fresh in the morning".
7. I know that my problem is that my costs are higher on the fresh fruit.
8. I know that I actually lost money. I decided to sell my "picked this week" fruit for 10 (profit=1) and my "picked fresh this morning" fruit for 13 (profit=3). I will try to upsell the freshly picked fruit to my customers.
9. I will get a partner or find an action partner.
10. I will look at my customer values from the previous page.
11. I will list my upsell products or services.
12. I will list my prices as shown below.

| UPSELL | MY UPSELL PRICES |
|---|---|
| I will sell fruit " picked fresh this morning". | Fruit " picked this week" price= 10 (profit of 1). Fruit " picked fresh this morning" price= 13 (profit of 2). |
| I will guarantee that laundry is done by 5:00 | Regular next-day laundry price= 20 (profit of 4). Guaranteed laundry price= 27 (profit of 8). |
| I will sell skin-care soap. | Regular soap price = 12 (profit of 2). Skin –care soap price=18 (profit of 6). |

After writing my ideas , I will share them with my business group.

HOW WILL I UPSELL?

1. I will find out the things that will make my customers buy more.
2. I will need an " upsell phrase".

3. I know that an upsell phrase could be; " It costs a little more, but -----".
4. I will fill in the blank with the value I know is important to the customer.
5. When my customers looked at the " picked this week" fruit , she says, " I have fruit picked fresh this morning".
6. I will add the upsell phrase , " it costs a little more , but it is fresher".
7. I will think of my own business.
8. I will think about the upsell items.
9. I will find out what I will say to upsell to my customers.
10. I will use the table below to create my upsell phrases .
11. I will provide examples.

WRITING AN UPSELL PHRASE

| FIRST PRODUCT OR SERVICE | UPSELL PRODUCT OR SERVICE | WHAT MY CUSTOMERS VALUE | UPSELL PHRASE |
| --- | --- | --- | --- |
| " Picked this week" fruit | "Picked fresh this morning" fruit | Quality (freshness) | It costs a little more, but it is fresher. |
| Half liter of milk for 3 | Liter of milk for 5 | Saving money | It costs a little more, but you get twice as much for only 2 more. |
| Regular soap | Skin- care soap | Quality | It costs a little more, but it is much better for your skin. |
| Laundry service | Press shirts | Saving time | It costs a little more, but it saves you a lot of time. |

Successful business owners make it easy to buy from them.

HOW WILL I SELL MY PRODUCTS MORE QUICKLY?

Successful business owners sell more to each customer so they can " turn inventory" quickly. To "turn inventory" means to sell all the products we bought from our suppliers. We can use upsell techniques to sell more to each customer. Successful business owners turn inventory often. Turn inventory quickly.

1. I know how to turn my inventory more quickly.
2. I know how turning inventory more quickly will increase my profits.

| BEFORE | WHAT I DID | AFTER |
|---|---|---|
| I paid my supplier 17 for a liter of milk. | I talked to my supplier about a discount when I buy in bulk. | I now pay 15 for a liter. |
| I increased my inventory with my bulk purchases. I did not change my prices. It took longer to turn my inventory and some of my milk went bad. | I used an upsell technique: if they buy two liters or more, they get a discount. | I now turn my inventory in two days. No milk spoils. I have the money to buy more. |

Some specialty products take a long time to sell, and that is okay. But, if we have products that simply are not selling, it means that our valuable business money is stuck in that inventory until it sells.

1. I will discuss with my action partner.
2. I will write down my ideas.
3. I will find out how I can turn my inventory more quickly.
4. I will find out how I can reduce the supply of inventory that simply is not selling.

HOW WILL I LOWER COSTS?

1. I know that turning inventory increases my profits.
2. I know that I can make my business more profitable by lowering expenses.
3. I will get an action partner.
4. We will take turns reading ways to reduce expenses below.
5. We will write other ways we can reduce expenses.

| FIXED | VARIABLE |
|---|---|
| Make do with what we have | Negotiate with suppliers |

| Rent | Use multiple suppliers. |

I will return to my business group and share my ideas.

HOW WILL I INCREASE PROFITS?

1. I will think of ways that I can avoid expenses.
2. I will think of using two helpers: James and John.
3. I will hire James to work at my fruit stand four hours every day (fixed cost).
4. I will not hire John, but I would only call him to make deliveries as needed (variable cost).
5. I will discuss with two other people about avoiding or reducing my fixed and variable costs.
6. I will list the variable and fixed costs of my business. I will get with a partner and discuss ways to reduce these costs.

WHAT SHOULD I DO TO IMPROVE?

1. I will counsel with the Lord in all my doings and he will direct me for good.
2. I will quietly ponder what I am learning.
3. I will write any impressions I have in my business notebook.
4. I will find the idea which will help my business the most this week.
5. I will make the idea my weekly business goal.
6. I will add my weekly business goal to my commitments.
7. I will share my weekly business goal and other impressions with other people.

HOW WILL I MAKE DAILY PROGRESS?

1. I will make and fulfill my commitments.
2. I will choose my action partner.
3. We shall decide when and how we will contact each other.
4. I will read each commitment aloud to my action partner.
5. I will promise to keep my commitments and sign my signature below.
   MY COMMITMENTS

1. I will try at least two ways to upsell with 10 or more customers.
2. I will try at least two ways to lower my fixed and variable costs.
3. I will achieve my weekly business goal.
4. I will practice the business principles and teach it to my family.
5. I will add to my savings- even a coin or two.
6. I will report to my action partner.

_____          _____
My signature                                            Action partner's signature.

HOW WILL I REPORT MY PROGRESS?

1. Before the next business meeting, I will use the commitment chart below to record my progress.
2. In the box below, I will write "Yes", "No", or the number of times I kept my commitment.

| Tried two ways to upsell with at least 10 customers (Write #). | Tried at least two ways to lower costs (Write #) | Achieved weekly business goal (Yes/ No) | Practiced business principles and taught it to my family (Yes/ No). | Added to my savings (Yes/ No) | Reported to action partner. (Yes / No) |
|---|---|---|---|---|---|
|  |  |  |  |  |  |

In my next business meeting, I will do self-reliance assessments again to see if I am becoming self –reliant.

MADE THE SALE, MISSED THE SALE

I will choose roles and act out the following:

JOHN: Hi, James. How are you today?

JAMES: Good, thank you. Who's your helper today?

JOHN: This is my nephew, Peter.

JAMES: What a good boy! Well, my brother found some work. He is still at my home, but he will help pay for food now.

JOHN: When did he start work?

JAMES: Just today!

JOHN: What a relief for him- and you!. So, what brings you here today?

JAMES: I'd like some more eggs. Everyone loved them and they saved us a lot. I 'd like eight more eggs and two jars of milk.

JOHN: Ok. Thanks for buying from me today, James. Have a great day!

PETER: She was carrying so many things. Why didn't you ask her to let you carry the eggs and milk for her?

JOHN: Oh, Peter. You are right. I should have thought of that. I had a chance to upsell a delivery service to her. I could have made 10 more on that sale.

THE UPSELL:

I will choose roles and act out the following:

JAMES: I'm back for eggs! And, I need 10 eggs today because I won't be able to come back for a few days.

JOHN: Great. I've been thinking about you. We have about the same number of mouths to feed and we eat at least 12 eggs. They're just so good for you.

JAMES: The problem is how to get them home. I actually broke two last time.

JOHN: I was worried about that. I can send Peter home with you to carry the eggs for you. We only charge 10 for delivery. It costs a little more, but it will save you the trouble of carrying them. Plus, if any break while Peter is delivering them, we will replace them for free.

JAMES: Well, you know, that would help. Okay , let's do that . Thank you.

JOHN: Sounds good. Peter, thank you for helping James. Hurry right back!

TURN INVENTORY QUICKLY

Choose roles and act out the following.

JOHN: Hi, James. What can I get for you today?

JAMES: I need some milk.

JOHN: Great. We have a lot.

JAMES: It's important to have enough for customers, but you also need to turn inventory quickly.

JOHN: Turn inventory? What does that mean?

JAMES: Turning inventory is selling everything you bought from your supplier.

JOHN: I try to turn my inventory, but sometimes it takes too long and I have to throw away the milk that has gone bad.

JAMES: So that's why you need to turn inventory quickly. Throwing away milk because you didn't sell it quickly is wasting your money. But that isn't the only reason you need to turn inventory quickly.

JOHN: Really?

JAMES: John, where does the money come from to pay your milk supplier.

JOHN: I save money from each milk sale. When I have enough, I buy more milk.

JAMES: John, the longer it takes you to turn inventory, the longer you have to wait to buy more milk. Remember, you only make money on a sale. So, the quicker you move your inventory, the more money you make. What would it be like if you could sell all your milk in three days? Or two days? Or even the same day?

JOHN: None of the milk would go bad, and I would be able to buy more from my supplier sooner. And I will have more milk to sell to my customers and I will make more money. I'm going to start turning my inventory more quickly.

MODULE 12: WEEK 12: HOW DO I CONTINUE TO IMPROVE MY BUSINESS.

( A ) STARTING AND GROWING MY BUSINESS.

1. I will facilitate a business meeting .
2. Today, my business group will spend extra 20 minutes in the commit section.
3. I will read the final activity.
4. I will be prepared to answer questions.
5. I will text or call all group members.
6. I will invite them to arrive 10 minutes early to report on their commitments.
7. I will prepare the meeting materials.
8. Thirty minutes before the meeting, I will set chairs around a table so everyone can be close.
9. I will draw this commitment chart on the board with the names of the people in my group as shown below:

| Group Member Name | Tried two ways to upsell with at least 10 customers. ( Write # of customers) | Tried at least two ways to lower costs (Write #) | Achieved weekly business goal (Yes/No) | Practiced business principle and taught it to my family. (Yes/ No) | Added to my savings. (Yes/ No). | Reported to action partner (Yes/ No). |
|---|---|---|---|---|---|---|
| John | 15 | 8 | Y | Y | Y | Y |

1. Ten minutes before the meeting, I will greet people warmly as they arrive.
2. As group members arrive, I will ask them to complete the commitment chart on the board.
3. I will remind them to update their progress towards certification.
4. I will ask of who completed their certification requirements.
5. I will sign a copy of the completion letter for each lesson who has completed the certificate.
6. After the meeting, the self- reliance committee will know who completed their certification requirements.

7. I will assign a timekeeper.
8. At starting time, ask people to turn off their phones and other devices.
9. I will have an opening prayer (and hymn , if desired).
10. I will set the timer to 20 minutes for my workbook and continue reading.
11. I will write what I learnt by keeping my commitments in my business notebook.

( C ) HOW DOES EVERYTHING FIT TOGETHER?

1. I will set the timer to 60 minutes.
2. We must believe in " We can do this".
3. My business is better than it was 12 weeks ago.
4. I will find out how my business is better than it was 12 weeks ago.
5. I will get with a group member.
6. I will get out my business success map.
7. I will find out how something from the map improved my business.
8. I will find out how multiple suppliers improved my business.
9. We will take turns asking each other questions for two minutes.
10. I believe we can do this.
11. I believe that we will have success.
12. We have started and will grow in our businesses.
13. We need to continue to improve our businesses and increase our profits.
14. I will find out how I will increase my profits.
15. I will continue learning and improving.
16. I will set goals for my business .
17. I will prepare a presentation about my business.

( D ) HOW WILL I REACH MY BUSINESS GOALS

1. I will fire my imagination and create excitement in my heart.
2. I will write three goals I have for my business in two minutes.
3. I will get with two other people.
4. I want to look at two goals shown below.
5. I want to get better at managing my money because often I don't have enough to pay for all my expenses unless I borrow from my family , which is sometimes difficult because they don't always have enough either.

6. I will double my profits next month.
7. I will find out the goal that is more exciting.
8. I will find the goal that is easier to measure (knowing when I have reached the goal).

Successful business owners set exciting measurable goals. Successful business owners set goals that are exciting, easy to remember, and easy to measure.

1. I will determine where I am in my business and what I need to do.
2. I will create inspiring, noble, and righteous goals that fire my imagination and create excitement in my heart.
3. I will keep my eye on them.
4. I will work consistently towards achieving them.
5. On my own, I will rewrite the three goals for my business.
6. I will take two minutes to make my goals exciting, easy to remember and easy to measure.
7. I will tell the person next to me about my most exciting goal.
8. I will move on to the next person until I have shared with everyone.
9. I will get back to my whole business group and share someone else's goal with the group and not my own.
10. I will find out if my goals don't just happen because we want them to happen. We have to work hard to achieve our goals.
11. I will write down my goals and what I plan to do to achieve them.
12. I will aim high, for I am capable of eternal blessings.

GOAL

I will double my profits next month by opening a stand on a busy street.

( E ) WHAT I WILL DO TO ACHIEVE THE GOAL.

1. I will have my son run my business while I look for a good place for my new stand.
2. I will give out samples so that people will know my products and buy from me.
3. I know that I will likely have difficulties and disappointments as I work on my goals.

4. I know that successful business owners never give up, and they plan ways to overcome difficulties ; example: John knew that most of his family members would criticize his business goals and say he could not achieve the goals. But he knew his uncle would be supportive. He planned to ask his uncle for advice and encouragement. He planned to pray for strength , kindness and patience. He planned to remain cheerful but determined when criticized.
5. I will share ideas of ways I can overcome difficulties in achieving my goals.
6. I will remember that the Lord will help me and that other people will help me.
7. I will write down my ideas.
8. I know that successful business owners never give up.
   ( F ) HOW DO I CONTINUE TO IMPROVE MY BUSINESS.
   HOW DO I PREPARE FOR GRADUATION.
1. As part of graduation, we will describe our businesses to other business owners, family members and friends.
2. I will follow along and present " My Business in Five Minutes" while everyone else follows along with the instructions.

( G ) MY BUSINESS IN FIVE MINUTES: INSTRUCTIONS.
1. In less than one minute, I will describe my business..
2. In less than one minute, I will describe how answering one of the following questions greatly improved my business.
a. What do people buy?
b. How do I sell?
c. How do I control costs?
d. How do I increase profits?
e. How do I run my business?
3. In less than one minute, I will describe how I will increase savings and keep financial records.
4. I will know how many weeks I added to my savings.
5. I will know how many weeks I will keep business financial records.
6. I will know how many weeks I will keep personal financial records.
7. In less than one minute, I will describe one thing I will do to continue improving my business.

8. In less than one minute, I will describe one business goal I have and how I will reach my goal.
9. During the week, I will think about what I would like to share as my ideas.
10. I will write my ideas in a business notebook.
11. I will practice giving my presentation to my family or friends.
12. I will come prepared to share my business presentations.
13. I can choose to use notes, charts , or other visual aids.

( H ) WHAT WILL I DO AFTER GRADUATION?

Several business owners learn continually. Successful business owners continually seek learning. We can learn from books, other business owners, classes, and each other. For example, I may consider registering my business. Discussing this with my group members or members of a business council can help me know when and how to do it.

1. I will like to continue meeting as a group.
2. I will like to meet with other groups in the business community.
3. If I choose to continue meeting, I will create my own agenda or follow an agenda like this:

(a ) My Foundation: Review of principles and topics.

(b) Report: Report on business progress and problems.

(c) Learn: Listen to speakers from local businesses, lenders, and government. Watch videos or read about business topics.

(d) Ponder: Reflect on what we are learning.

( e ) Commit: Choose goals and make commitments.

( I ) AM I BECOMING SELF- RELIANT?

1. My goal is self-reliance, both temporal and spiritual. Making my business succeed is only part of that goal. I am on my part to self-reliant.
2. I will list the changes that I have seen in my life as I practiced and taught the My Foundation Principles.

3. I will assess my path to self-reliance. I will complete the steps.
4. When I am done, I will take three minutes to ponder on whether I am now more aware of my expenses.
5. I can now answer "often" or "always" to many more questions.
6. I am now more confident in the amount I have set as my self-reliant income.
7. I will ponder on what to do to improve.

( J ) PONDER: WHAT SHOULD I DO TO IMPROVE?

1. I will set the timer to 10 minutes for the ponder section.
2. I know that verily, men should be anxiously engaged in a good cause, and do many things of their own free will, and bring to pass much righteousness.
3. I will ponder on what I am learning.
4. I will write the impressions I have in my business notebook.
5. I will identify the idea that will help my business the most this week.
6. I will make this idea, my weekly business goal.
7. I will add my weekly business goal to my commitments.
8. I will share my weekly business goal and other impressions.

( K ) COMMIT: HOW WILL I MAKE DAILY PROGRESS?

1. I will set the timer to 10 minutes for this page only.
2. I will read each commitment aloud to a partner.
3. I will promise to keep my commitments and sign below.

MY COMMITMENTS

1. I will prepare a presentation about my business.
2. I will set goals for my business.
3. I will achieve my weekly business goal.
4. I will achieve today's foundation principles and teach it to my family.
5. I will add to my savings- even a coin or two each week.

_____

My Signature

( L ) HOW CAN I CONTINUE BEING SELF- RELIANT?

1. I will set the timer to 20 minutes for this page.
2. I will do my final activity and plan a service project as a group.
3. I will congratulate myself because the Lord has blessed me with new knowledge and skills and I have accomplished great things.
4. I will keep my business momentum going.
5. I will volunteer and serve at a self-reliance center near me.
6. I know that one purpose of becoming self- reliant is to be able to help others.
7. I know that serving others is a great blessing.
8. I will continue with my business group and continue to support and encourage each other.
9. I will continue attending self-reliance devotionals.
10. I will keep in contact with my action partner. We will support and encourage each other.
11. I will continue to progress by making and keeping commitments.

_____

My signature

( M ) WE CAN DO THIS !

I will choose roles and act out the following:

JOHN: Wow, this really works! I finally see it.

JAMES: What are you talking about? What works?

JOHN: Everything fits together. Twelve weeks ago, when we started going to our self-reliance group, I had no idea how much it would improve our business. The commitments we've been keeping, the things we've learned in our self-reliance group- it all makes sense!

JAMES: Yes, I have found the same with my job search self- reliance group. I now have a great job at the hospital. With the income from my job and your egg business, we will finally be able to provide for our family. Everything does fit.

JOHN: James, it's not just my business. It's our business. Thank you for working so hard at your job and then helping me with our egg business.

JAMES: It's also the Lord's business. We've consecrated our business efforts to him, exercised faith in the savior, and prayed about our business.

JOHN: We needed to look very closely at our egg business. We talked to customers and other business owners to figure out what people wanted. Remember ! We realized that we should sell milk with our eggs.

JAMES: Yes, and we looked at where we get our eggs and milk. We decided that it wasn't a good idea for us to get a goat for milk . It is better to buy fresh milk from Andrew, who already has several goats.

JOHN: Then we learned how to make money everyday. I have been keeping track of everything we are spending and how much people pay us. We made a lot more money when we started doing home delivery.

JAMES: And I have also been tracking how much we are spending and how much we are making for our family. We can pay for the kid's school supplies now.

JOHN: Mark helped us figure out how to sell more. We started asking our customers questions, listening to them, and making suggestions. We encouraged customers to buy more eggs and to buy milk. That was a great idea to send Peter for home delivery. We got to know our customers better and became friends with many of them.

JAMES: Then , with all the customers, we needed more eggs every day, and we learned about borrowing money to get more chickens . I am glad we didn't get that first loan. We would not have been able to make payments.

We just needed a small loan to buy a few more chickens.

JOHN: See! It all fits together. Now we just need to keep looking at ways to reduce our costs and increase how much we sell.

JAMES: Yes, we can do this.

MY BUSINESS IN FIVE MINUTES

I will read the following while the other business group members follow along.

JOHN: I'm a little nervous to present but I have gotten to know you all as well. I'm going to be ok.

Part 1: I'm supposed to describe my business. My business is selling eggs and milk. I started with just eggs a few months ago. I added milk after I learned that my customers wanted it. I also have a home-delivery service now. My business is doing much better since I have been going to this self- reliance group.

JOHN: Part 2 is about the questions of the week. The questions have all helped me. But if I had to choose one, the question that improved my business the most was separating business and personal finances.

Before that, any money I made in my business got mixed with my personal money and was spent. It wasn't good. Now I keep them separate.

JOHN: Part 3- financial records and savings. I was able to save money 9 of the 12 weeks. I kept financial records for my business for the last 8 weeks straight. I did the same for my personal records. I plan on continuing to keep records. I really like knowing how much I make and how much I spend.

I am also very happy to have money in savings. I have never had that before. It comforts me to know that it is there.

JOHN: Ok, now for part 4-continuing to improve my business. I have learned so much in the past 12 weeks. I want to continue to learn. I am going to join other business owner's group.

JOHN: Last part. Part 5 is a business goal. In one year, I want my business to have enough cash flow that I can rent a space in the busiest part of the market. That will help me grow my business even more. Thanks , everyone.

You have really helped me improve my business.

( N ) AM I PROGRESSING TOWARDS MY CERTIFICATE?

Each week, I will track how well I am progressing towards my International Business Entrepreneurship Certificate (IBEC).

Put a check mark in each box as you attend the group meetings and keep commitments.

BUSINESS ENTREPRENEURSHIP REQUIREMENTS

| Week | Attended 10 group meetings | Kept personal and business financial records for 8 weeks. | Added money to savings for 10 weeks | Kept weekly business goal for 10 weeks. | Made a business presentation |
|---|---|---|---|---|---|
| 1 | | | | | |
| 2 | | | | | |
| 3 | | | | | |
| 4 | | | | | |
| 5 | | | | | |
| 6 | | | | | |
| 7 | | | | | |
| 8 | | | | | |
| 9 | | | | | |
| 10 | | | | | |
| 11 | | | | | |
| 12 | | | | | |
| Total | | | | | |

(O) **LETTER OF COMPLETION**

To Whom It May Concern:

_____has participated in a self-reliance group called " Starting and Growing My Business" provided by Philip Nelson Business School, and has fulfilled the requirements necessary for completion as follows:

Attended at least 10 meetings      --------of 12.

Kept personal and business financial records for 8 weeks .---------of 8.

Added money to savings for at least 10 weeks.    -----------of 12.

Kept weekly business goal for at least 10 weeks. -------of 12.

Made my business presentation to the group (Circle one)  Yes or No.

_____   _____   _____

Facilitator name              Facilitator Signature          Date

I have practiced and built a foundation of skills , principles and habits for self-reliance. I will continue to use this throughout my life.

_____   _____   _____

Group member name     Group member signature     Date

NOTE: An International Business Entrepreneurship Certificate (IBEC) from Philip Nelson Business School (PNBS) , will be issued at a later date by the self-reliance committee.

( P ) BUSINESS SUCCESS MAP

Principles for Business Success.

1. CUSTOMERS: What do people want to buy?
- Know why people buy your product.
- Know what customers value.
- Learn from customers daily.
2. COSTS: How can I control costs?
- Lower costs.
- Use multiple suppliers.
- Only add fixed costs when they will increase profits.
- Make investments wisely.
3. SALES: How do I sell?
- Always upsell .
- Turn inventory often.
- Ask, listen, suggest.
- Make it easy to buy.
- Close the sale.

4. PROFIT: How do I increase profits?
- Keep daily records.
- Pay yourself a salary.
- Seek daily profit.
- Buy low, sell high.
- Don't steal from your business.
- Use productive assets.

(5) BUSINESS SUCCESS: How do I run my business?

- Separate personal and personal records.
- Keep daily records.
- Pay tithing first.
- Save weekly.
- Improve something every day.
- Learn continually.
- Live the foundation principles.
- Set exciting, measurable goals.
- Start small, think big.
- Never give up!.

(Q) PHILIP NELSON BUSINESS SCHOOL ONLINE.

Offers complete practical business and professional online training on Starting and Growing Your Business leading to the award of an International Business Entrepreneurship Certificate in business entrepreneurship covering such topics such as:

- How do I start or improve my business?
- What do people want to buy?
- How do I buy my product and set the sales price?
- How do I know if my business is making profit?
- How do I separate my business and family money?
- How is my business progressing?
- How will I grow my business?
- How much can I afford to invest to grow my business?

- How will I attract more customers and close sales?
- How will I increase my profits?
- How do I continue to improve my business?
  Certificate will be issued.
  **For further information, contact: philipanochie@gmail.com.**

www.ingramcontent.com/pod-product-compliance
Lightning Source LLC
Chambersburg PA
CBHW021453210526
45463CB00002B/765